Deciphering the
Diagnostic Codes

Practical Skills for Counselors
Jeffrey A. Kottler, Series Editor

W. Paul Jones

Deciphering the Diagnostic Codes

A Guide for School Counselors

CORWIN PRESS, INC.
A Sage Publications Company
Thousand Oaks, California

For information address:

Corwin Press
A Sage Publications Company.
2455 Teller Road
Thousand Oaks, California 91320
E-mail: order@sagepub.com

SAGE Publications Ltd.
6 Bonhill Street
London EC2A 4PU
United Kingdom

SAGE Publications India Pvt. Ltd.
M-32 Market
Greater Kailash I
New Delhi 110048 India

Printed in the United States of America

Library of Congress Cataloging-in-Publication Data

Jones, W. Paul.
   Deciphering the diagnostic codes : a guide for school counselors /
author, W. Paul Jones.
     p. cm. — (Practical skills for counselors)
   Includes index.
   ISBN 0-8039-6473-0 (pbk.). — ISBN 0-8039-6472-2 (cloth)
   1. Mental illness—Diagnosis. 2. Child psychopathology.
3. Adolescent psychopathology. 4. Educational counseling.
I. Title. II. Series.
RJ503.5.J66 1997
618.92'89075—dc21   96-51223

This book is printed on acid-free paper.
97 98 99 00 01 02 03 10 9 8 7 6 5 4 3 2 1

Editorial Assistant:	Kristen L. Green
Production Editor:	Sherrise M. Purdum
Production Assistant:	Denise Santoyo
Typesetter/Designer:	Danielle Dillahunt
Cover Designer:	Marcia R. Finlayson
Indexer:	Teri Greenberg
Print Buyer:	Anna Chin

Contents

Preface

Why Is This Book Needed?

"What we've got here is a failure to communicate." This line from a classic movie could be the defining feature in many counseling interventions. In this case, however, it is why this book was written and the reason why the content is essential for a contemporary practice in school counseling.

For better or for worse, diagnostic coding is increasingly assimilated into all facets of the counseling profession. Communication among counselors and other professionals who work in the arena of mental health assumes an ease and facility with the diagnostic concepts to a much greater extent than is often emphasized in counselor education programs. The intent of this book is to facilitate the communication, to enhance your understanding and use of the diagnostic codes.

With each new edition of the *Diagnostic and Statistical Manual of Mental Disorders* (*DSM*), your mailbox is filled with announcements of workshops, guidebooks, and other training opportunities. Notably absent in those materials, however, has been a recognition of the existence of the school counselor. You have more contact with more children and adolescents than probably any other human service professionals. The content and the focus in available materials, however, are directed elsewhere, and that is the problem that stimulated the writing of this book.

What you find inside is a balance between the general and the specific. This book is not a handbook for use of the *DSM* or any other specific model. It is instead a focused guide that will make it easier to use any of the diagnostic systems.

We will examine the features that result in the diagnosis of a specific condition, only periodically illustrating with the specific numerical code. Knowing what a diagnosis is supposed to communicate about the problems being faced by a student makes it a simple matter, then, to translate to any numerical code.

Who Should Read This Book?

This book was written by someone with experience as a school counselor and specifically for an audience of school counselors. After the introductory material, we examine the diagnosis of various conditions, with the order of the chapters generally determined by how likely you are to see a student who has that condition. Examples of the disorders are presented that illustrate applications in the practice of school counseling.

The material in this book will reinforce many concepts you learned in your preparation for school counseling. The content will sharpen your skills in use of those concepts with the vocabulary of the diagnostic codes.

What's in This Book

We begin our tour with an overview of the basic ideas and terminology used in diagnosis. This is followed by a chapter devoted to multiaxial coding. A frequent misperception about diagnosis is the belief that there is insufficient attention to the context in which a student's distress may occur. As you will see in Chapter 2, this perception could hardly be further from the truth. In fact, multiaxial (multidimensional) diagnostic coding is designed specifically to give major consideration to all features that could be contributing to a student's distress.

Then, in a sequence based on likelihood of your encountering the disorders, we begin examination of the specific conditions of distress. Chapter 3 is devoted to what are often referred to as *V codes,* conditions for which counseling is needed even though the problems are technically not mental disorders. In Chapter 4, we examine the conditions for which there is an identified cause for the distress: the adjustment disorders. Both of these chapters include discussion and examples of how issues related to managed care and third-party payment can influence the assignment of a diagnosis.

In Chapters 5 and 6, we move to the more serious conditions, first anxiety and then depressive disorders. In addition to examination of the general criteria used to make a diagnosis of one or more of these disorders, these chapters include discussion both of how the conditions may be identified in the school-age population and of implications for intervention.

Although we may more often think of mental disorders coming from the affective domain, diagnostic coding systems also include problems associated with the cognitive domain. What are known as academic disorders are examined in Chapter 7. Furor and controversy surrounding the diagnosis of attention-deficit/hyperactivity disorder warrants a specific chapter. With some trepidation, in Chapter 8, we will make an excursion into the science and the politics of the attention disorders.

The diagnostic conditions in any of these chapters may be found in both children and adolescents. Chapter 9, however, is specifically devoted to problems of adolescence that often come to the attention of secondary school counselors.

The final chapter serves several purposes. It provides a brief summary and suggestions for obtaining information about the disorders not included. The chapter includes discussion about alternative models of diagnostic systems, both advantages and possible limitations. The chapter also addresses a philosophical issue: *What if* use of the diagnostic codes were to become a requirement in communication within the school counseling specialty?

As we go through the primary concepts in diagnosis, you will encounter instances of a wonderfully logical system, which also includes some classifications that seem to absolutely defy common sense. You will find explanation of how diagnostic coding systems are designed to be used, spiced occasionally with examples of one practitioner's view of how systems are sometimes bent to comply with outside pressures.

What's Not in This Book?

A conscious decision was made to avoid the continuing reference citations typical in most textbooks. The Appendix includes some basic resources that you may find helpful. The opinions are my own; and the occasional noting of prevalence rates can be confirmed (or disputed) in the resources listed in the Appendix.

Every attempt has been made to avoid a pitfall that often seems evident in diagnostic resources. To meet the goal of being comprehensive, many guides can be overwhelming, replete with information that either is not especially relevant or would be self-evident to anyone with at least three digits in his or her latest IQ score.

This book makes no claim to be a comprehensive compendium of all possible information. Rare and esoteric conditions are not included. When the underlying concepts of diagnosis are mastered, it is easy to look up those conditions in the encyclopedic manuals.

This book is intended as a conversation, as if we are talking together as colleagues about the use of diagnostic coding systems. The only difference in this case (and some of my colleagues might suggest that this isn't much of a difference) is that I get to do all the talking.

Acknowledgments

The list of persons who contributed to the information shared in this book would exceed the length of the book itself. Recognition is due my university colleagues, particularly Jeffrey Kottler, who is editing this series and with whom I have shared thoughts, argued ideas, and publicly debated the merits of the diagnostic systems.

Also acknowledged are both colleagues and clients in the mental health arena. Over the years, they have helped me to better understand the realities of diagnosis in the real world.

My three daughters, Donna, Cindy, and Jann, have been a continuing inspiration (sometimes helping me truly understand what anxiety really means). My three granddaughters, Alicia, Kari, and Christy, provide an essential reminder for anyone who works in this field that some children are happy, healthy, and without a disorder.

Special recognition is due my wife, Dorothy, also a professional in human services. She has contributed inspiration, understanding, and ideas (and also a great deal of tolerance as, over the past several months, I regularly disappeared into the world of the computer).

About the Author

W. Paul Jones (Ph. D) is Professor and Chair of the Department of Educational Psychology at the University of Nevada, Las Vegas. His professional publications include more than 30 journal articles, a textbook in educational psychology, a nationally standardized achievement test for students with visual disability, cassette tape programs, and computer-assisted learning packages. At the university, he teaches courses in measurement and counseling appraisal, and his honors include college and university awards for exemplary teaching and research. Professional associations include the American Counseling Association, the American Psychological Association, and the National Academy of Neuropsychology. He began his career as a public school teacher and then a school counselor in New Mexico. He is a licensed psychologist and has had either full- or part-time practice for the past 20 years. Although now a full-time academician, he maintains a diagnostic practice in conjunction with a nearby hospital. Diagnostics is thus more than an area of academic content; it is a tool he uses almost daily in preparation of reports based on assessment of children, adolescents, and adults.

1

Diagnosis
COMMUNICATION AND CREDIBILITY

Why should you care about diagnostic terminology that might at first glance appear more relevant for professionals whose specialty is something other than school counseling? Why invest the time in learning to decipher the codes? Does this really matter?

Diagnostic coding in the practice of school counseling can enhance communication about the problems faced by the students we serve. The codes, when used correctly, can lead to more appropriate and effective assistance for the students. Diagnostic codes are clearly applicable when providing individual or group counseling, but the potential application goes even further. When you design a group guidance activity or prepare an instructional unit, the objective is to resolve (or prevent) problems. Diagnostic codes define those problems.

Communication and Diagnosis:
Let's Talk

A part of the answer to the does-this-really-matter question may be found in the following scene:

> Your phone rings, and the person calling you is a local mental health professional to whom you have referred a 15-year-old student. After introductory pleasantries are finished, the therapist tells you that the parents have signed a release of information form and requested that you specifically be informed of the outcome of the therapist's evaluation of this student. The parents are concerned about increasingly poor academic performance, noting that you seem to be the only person the student trusts in the school setting. The therapist tells you that there is time in this conversation only for a quick overview of the findings.
>
> Everything is okay so far. You also understand the pressures of time and are likely to have either a student waiting, a report overdue, or a class waiting for your arrival. The therapist then proceeds to tell you that there were insufficient indicators to warrant identification of generalized anxiety on Axis I, but there was sufficient evidence for a 309.24. The therapist goes on to say that you should be aware that there were clear borderline indicators on Axis II, and that the GAF is 55. Promising that a complete psychological report will be mailed to you as soon as it is available and that the therapist will really appreciate your help with this student and the parents, the therapist ends the conversation.

Faced with a scenario like this, what would you do? If you are comfortable with diagnostic terminology, you have just received a great deal of information about this student. But what if you are not? What is a 309.24? How can something be both clear and borderline? And what in the world is a GAF?

It would not be wise to assume that these points would be clarified in the full psychological report. First, it may be weeks before the report actually arrives. Speaking as one who writes them, psychological evaluations are seldom clear, often verbose, and typically assume a great deal of prior knowledge. (That's not how they should be, but unfortunately that's how they usually are.)

We tend to universally tout the value of the team approach in assisting persons who have problems. Our profession-specific vocabularies and acronyms, however, create major stumbling blocks in actually creating effectively functioning teams.

Shared use and understanding of a common diagnostic coding system can relieve at least some of the communication problems. We will continue to have both inter- and intraprofessional differences about what caused a problem for the individual and how that problem should be addressed. Diagnostic coding systems allow us, however, to have a common shared understanding about what the problem is. The pattern of personal distress and impaired performance identified with a specific code is the same whether the problem is being addressed by a professional school counselor, a clinical social worker, a psychologist, or a physician.

Credibility and the Diagnosis:
Let's Get Real

Continuing with the case of the referred student, it's now later on that same day:

Still puzzled about what the therapist meant in that strange conversation, you have had many other things to do and have decided you can check this out with a colleague when you have time. Then, the student aide announces that you have unexpected visitors.

They are the parents of that 15-year-old. They are obviously distraught and tell you that they really need your help. The therapist went over the psychological evaluation with them. They didn't understand most of what was said but knew that you could help them.

Obviously, unless you are comfortable with the terminology used in the diagnostic codes, this is not turning out to be a good day. If you are at ease with the terminology in the codes, you have an opportunity to help both the parents and the student. If not, you have a dilemma about how honest to be with them. You can admit that you also don't understand diagnostic terminology. That's laudable but isn't going to help your credibility when you have other suggestions to make to the parents. You could try to fake your way through it, but that's dishonest and unethical (and besides you'll probably get caught). You could give the speech you heard in class about the dangers of the medical model. That might be tempting, but remember, you made the referral to this therapist, and if successful in your own defense, you would be undermining the therapist's ability to be of help to the student. Like some multiple-choice questions, there doesn't seem to be a good choice unless you know the terminology.

The two Cs, communication and credibility, are the primary reasons why diagnostic coding systems are important for the school counselor. Your understanding of the coding systems facilitates your communication with other professionals. On occasion, your facility with the codes can also have a dramatic impact on your credibility.

Developmental Guidance and Diagnosis: War or Peace

When counselor educators are asked to define what school counselors should be doing, developmental guidance or comprehensive guidance (or comprehensive developmental guidance) is a safe prediction for the answer. By whatever name, there is emphasis on responsive services, typically with sequentially presented activities that target whole student growth and development. The words *development* and *developmental* permeate descriptions of the optimal school counseling practice in textbooks, accreditation manuals, and conference presentations.

There are, of course, good reasons for this emphasis. The idea behind the developmental model is, among other things, to communicate that school counselors use a variety of tools, not just the individual counseling session, and to communicate that school counseling programs are intended to prevent problems, not just treat them.

Suggestions of irreconcilable differences between the objectives of developmental guidance and the use of diagnostic coding systems, unfortunately, appear at times to have attained the status of essential truths. Alleged incompatibility can be such a pervasive belief that questions about the specific claims of incompatibility are dismissed with verbiage, suggesting that no answer is necessary.

Models of developmental guidance and models of diagnostic coding certainly appear different. The question is whether the difference is more apparent than real. Consider, for example, *prevention* as a stated goal in developmental guidance. Prevention of problems is an admirable objective but is not very specific. Prevention of what problems?

Diagnostic codes allow the addition of an important specificity in answer to that question. The focus is different, but the objectives are complementary, not adversarial.

A belief that diagnostic codes serve only to label students would also suggest some incompatibility between the objectives of developmental guidance and the use of diagnostic coding. It is true that suggesting another human being *is* a 296.32 is demeaning and dehumanizing. However, to report that he or she is experiencing moderate symptoms of distress with a major, recurrent, depressive disorder conveys a great deal of information. In the primary diagnostic coding system, that information is conveyed with a simple code, 296.32.

The critical phrasing is that one *has* rather than one *is*. The former describes a condition that presently exists. The latter ascribes this as a state of being. Diagnostic coding is intended simply to describe what *someone has* in a manner to increase precision of communication.

Defining the Terms

The thesaurus defines *diagnosis* as a noun that is an expression of a conclusion or an opinion. Do school counselors draw conclusions and have informed opinions about the needs of the students they serve? The obvious answer suggests that, regardless of what it is called, the process of diagnosis is a part of what school counselors do.

There is no intent to suggest that training as a school counselor is incomplete unless it results in competence to provide diagnosis for all manner and type of distress and impairment that plague the human condition. Aside from the fact that I have yet to meet anyone with any type of training that results in such global capability, differential diagnosis of mental disorders is not a reasonable objective for work requirements of the school counselor. The point here, though, is that this is an appropriate outcome of division of labor, not the result of the concepts underlying diagnosis being part of some evil empire.

There are professionals quite competent in some areas of differential diagnosis who would be hopelessly lost if confronted with the responsibility of counseling a group of children or adolescents in a school. There are school counselors who, by virtue of interest and experience, are quite capable of very precise and accurate diagnosis, particularly in regard to the conditions most often seen in the school setting.

Over the years, we have often demonstrated an unfortunate tendency to substitute new terms when we are uncomfortable with semantic connotations of terms introduced by related professional groups. The use of the terms *assessment* and *appraisal* to substitute for the term *diagnosis* may be one good example.

The intent may have been only to encourage more descriptive terminology or to seek stronger professional identity. The outcome, too often, has been only to impede communication among related professional groups. When new terminology is used to define something other than, broader than, the drawing of a conclusion, the new term is potentially helpful. Simply attempting to eliminate a term because it came from another professional group, though, seems highly counterproductive.

The primary intent of diagnostic coding systems is to be descriptive. The goal is to create a common language for communication among professionals. A person seeks help because of a feeling of distress. That person could seek help from someone with a strong commitment to a family systems approach. Assistance could be sought from someone committed to behavior modification. The mental health professional could, in fact, have a strong commitment to use of psychopharmacology.

Obviously, the kind of help given to the person would probably be very different among these three professionals, and they would also likely have a different view of what caused the problem. In a diagnostic coding system, however, these three professionals would be expected to come together on the description of the condition that led that person to seek assistance. Differences are in *why* and *how* to help. Commonality is expected in the *what*.

By definition, a *mental disorder* is a pattern of behavior that results in the individual experiencing significant degrees of distress or difficulty in coping with essential functions in daily living. Behavior is broadly defined to include thoughts and feelings as well as overt actions. Essential function is broadly defined to include interactions with others, school or occupational success, and so forth. In addition, the term *mental disorder* is used in coding systems to include patterns of behavior, which may not now be creating distress or impaired function but which significantly increase the risk of such an outcome.

The term *mental disorder* has been retained in diagnostic coding systems simply because a better term has not emerged. As you read the descriptions associated with various conditions, you may or may not be comfortable with calling that condition a mental disorder. The beauty of diagnostic coding is that there is no implicit or explicit requirement that you do so.

For example, we know that children can experience significant distress when parents are in the process of separation or divorce. We know that the distress can reach a level that creates major problems for the child in academics, in interpersonal relationships, and in social development. A diagnostic coding system provides a tool for that child's individual condition to be described, including the level of severity, the influence of environmental factors, and so forth. A counselor can use the coding to communicate specifics of the condition with or without personal belief that the child's condition should be termed as a mental disorder.

Because a primary goal of diagnosis is to improve communication, the term *mental disorder* will not, however, be consciously avoided. In like manner, the term *symptom* will also be used frequently. A symptom is generally understood to simply be something that signals the existence of something else.

There was, however, one term that did create some dilemma. As you know, there is a long history of struggle to identify the exact point of demarcation for what is *counseling* and what is *psychotherapy*. Any attempt at resolution of that issue goes far beyond the scope of this book (and is actually irrelevant for the understanding of diagnostic coding).

There is some potential awkwardness, though, in that the term *counseling* is seldom used for some of the conditions that will be described, and making a selection of a term according to the severity of the condition would seem to be unintentionally taking a side on the counseling versus psychotherapy question. To avoid this dilemma, *intervention* is used as a generic term for the service provided to help relieve the distress or enhance the development of the client.

Preview of Things to Come

The intent of this book is to provide a helpful resource for your practice in school counseling. Conspicuously absent will be the frequent reference citations you've come to expect in journal articles.

The dominant diagnostic coding system, *The Diagnostic and Statistical Manual of Mental Disorders* (*DSM*), was developed by the American Psychiatric Association, and there is periodic suggestion from some counselors, psychologists, and social workers that their professional associations should develop and use unique coding systems.

The decision in this book to typically illustrate using the framework of the *DSM* was easy to make. It is without question the most widely used system for classification of the kinds of problems associated with the practice of school counseling. Whether the *DSM* is the "best" is not at issue here. It is ubiquitous.

This book, though, is not intended as a *DSM* guide. The specific number codes will seldom be mentioned. Instead, for the conditions most likely to be encountered in a school setting, we will explore the concepts of diagnosis. Our exploration begins in the next chapter, with an examination of a broad-based perspective in diagnosis: multiaxial coding.

Multiaxial Assessment
FROM THE BOTTOM UP

Although there are many different systems for diagnosis, without question the most widely used is the *Diagnostic and Statistical Manual (DSM)*. It was initially a tool used only by physicians; mental problems were viewed as medical problems. The manual has been periodically updated, and each revision has broadened the perspective and increased the number of professional groups who provide guidance in its design and content.

The third edition of the *DSM* began use of a concept referred to as *multiaxial,* an interesting term that simply means that a diagnostic assessment of an individual should include more than just the attachment of a single label. An *axis* in this case is a dimension that is addressed in the diagnostic assessment. It could easily be argued that the addition of multidimensional considerations was a feature that dramatically increased the appropriateness of this historical diagnostic model for use in school settings by counselors.

In everyday activity, it is typical to consider multiple dimensions when assessing a person or a situation. When you walk into a room, for example, the automatic response is to observe more than just the size of the room. Multiaxial scaling is thus intuitively consistent with typical information-processing activity.

The multiaxial system is intended to provide a portrait of the person being evaluated, using several dimensions. There is consideration of the possible presence of a mental disorder or other condition that warrants intervention and, if found, an identification of the condition (Axis I). More pervasive features are also evaluated, features that may either contribute to the Axis I disorder or instead be *the* disorder for which intervention is required (Axis II). The diagnostic process is incomplete without attention to the possible influence of medical conditions that either may be contributing to a mental disorder or must be considered in planning an intervention (Axis III). The possible influence of psychosocial features on the disorder or on optimal intervention (Axis IV) is another component in a multiaxial evaluation. In addition, there is a general assessment of how well the individual is now functioning (Axis V). Table 2.1 illustrates a multiaxial evaluation for the case discussed in Chapter 1.

Our explanation of the multiaxial dimensions begins *at the end*, with Axis V, the present functioning level. The reverse order may at first seem peculiar but in fact reflects the process actually used by most diagnosticians.

We look first at how well the person is now functioning and then search for psychosocial stressors that could account for a problem in function. This is followed by exploration of possible contributing medical conditions. Consideration is then given to whether there are more general personality features that must be included to understand the problem and then, finally, there is identification of the problem itself.

Axis V: The Quantitative Answer to, How Are You?

Assume that you have just completed a counseling session with one of your students. You have a decision to make. Do you need to

TABLE 2.1 Example of Multiaxial Evaluation

Axis I	309.24	Adjustment Disorder/Anxious Mood
Axis II	301.83	Borderline Personality Disorder
Axis III		No Apparent Contribution
Axis IV		Educational Problems—Failing Grades
Axis V	GAF = 55	(current)

schedule another appointment with this student? Do you need to make a referral to a mental health professional? Is there information about this student that should be shared with a teacher? the parents?

Your answers to these questions are determined in part by how well you think the student is now able to cope. Your evaluation, in the terminology of *DSM* diagnostic coding on Axis V, is called the Global Assessment of Functioning (GAF). The GAF probably differs from what you already do only in that the perception is reported as a number on a scale of 1 to 100, the higher the number, the better the functioning. Table 2.2 is an abbreviated version of a GAF scale.

GAF categories are provided in groups of 10. For example, a score between 91 and 100 indicates that the person is doing exceptionally well, with no evident symptoms of poor adjustment or disorder. If the only problems are occasional arguments with others, or perhaps being slightly nervous before an exam, the GAF would be between 81 and 90. A student worried about an upcoming move who, as a result, was not keeping up with the work in school might receive a GAF between 71 and 80.

As a rule of thumb, if the GAF level is 70 or below, you will want to seek assistance from another professional, either for a referral or to confirm your assessment. Mild symptoms, such as occasional truancy or stealing from family members, are examples of symptoms usually assigned a GAF between 61 and 70. Moderate symptoms, for instance, occasional panic attacks, are assigned a GAF between 51 and 60. Serious symptoms include frequent thoughts of suicide; they would result in a GAF between 41 and 50. Table 2.2 stops at this level. It is likely that the students with whom you will have the most contact will be at the upper end of the GAF scale.

The complete scale, however, continues with symptoms of increasing severity. The lower ends of the scale describe persons who, at the

TABLE 2.2 Abbreviated Scale of General Adaptive Function

Number Scale	Verbal Description
91-100	No distress symptoms
81-90	Few distress symptoms
71-80	Some distress but within normal range
61-70	Mild distress but outside normal range
51-60	Moderate distress
41-50	Serious distress

NOTE: Scores below 71 indicate a probable need for referral. Scores below 41 indicate severe, typically psychotic, disorder. A score of 0 is used when information for GAF is not available.

moment, are at extreme risk to themselves or others. A 0 is used when there is insufficient information to make the assessment (which would be a very rare occurrence).

The GAF number is followed in parentheses by an identifying frame of reference. In most instances, as in the example in Table 2.1, the designation will be "current."

At one time, it was the norm for all evaluations to include two indications of GAF, one for the current level and another to represent the highest level during the previous year. The contrast between these two numbers provided information that could be significant. A student whose present level of functioning as described with the GAF scale was 70, and whose highest level during the preceding year was 75, presents a quite different challenge from one whose GAF had fallen from 90 to 70 during the year.

The highest level during the preceding year, however, is now seldom reported on the evaluations. The value of the contrast has apparently been overridden by the reality that the examiner often did not have sufficient social history to make more than just a guess at the level of highest functioning during the prior year.

If you are reviewing a hospital record, you may find two designations: "at admission" and "at discharge." It is in the hospital's best interest, of course, for there to be evident improvement between admission and discharge, so any instances in which the discharge level is not higher than the admission level are noteworthy.

When interpreting the GAF in multiaxial evaluation, it is also important to remember that within each 10-point category, the actual number assigned may reflect as much about the evaluator as it does about the evaluatee. Some mental health professionals routinely use the entire scale, for example, reporting GAFs of 71, 72, 73, and so on. Some will instead typically use only one number within each category, for example, reporting only 60, 70, 80, and so on. For most, the norm appears to be use of the numbers in multiples of 5, for example, reporting GAFs of 60, 65, 70, 75, and so on. Specific questionnaires exist to identify the GAF for the report, but most use a general history to suggest the numerical score.

In all cases, the GAF number will typically represent only one person's assessment of the present functioning level, and it is important that you not overestimate the precision of that estimate. At the same time, the GAF on a psychological evaluation does provide you with another person's view of the student, and that can be important information.

Your view, as well as that of the other professional, is affected by the setting in which it was obtained. Knowing, for example, that a student, who is meeting all of the criteria to be a "holy terror" in the school setting, is able in other settings to either stop or hide those behaviors is extremely valuable as you plan how you should best work with that student.

Above all else, the GAF scale is simply a shorthand tool for professionals to communicate their perceptions about the severity of a person's present condition. In the case presented in Chapter 1 and illustrated in Table 2.1, a GAF of 55 was reported by the consulting mental health professional. Even with no other information, the professional has communicated to you a belief that there was no apparent present suicide risk, that impairment in ability to cope was more than would be expected from ordinary stressors, and that the impairment was having sufficient impact on the student's present ability to cope to warrant some therapeutic intervention. The professional could, of course, have simply told you that information without using a number. On the other hand, with use of just a single number, a lot of information was presented rather efficiently.

Axis IV:
What's Been Going On?

When interpreting a report prepared using the multiaxial model, it is helpful to remember that the primary areas of focus are Axis I and Axis II. These provide the evaluator's decisions about whether there is evidence of mental disorder(s) and, if so, what the disorder(s) may be. Axis IV is designed to provide a part of the context for the identified disorder(s). Axis IV is used to indicate environmental and social features that may have contributed to the problems being presented by the student. These features are typically reported in broad categories, only occasionally describing the specific events. For example, Axis IV may report "problems with primary support group." The example in Table 2.1 identifies "educational problems" on Axis IV. The instructions for Axis IV suggest identification of both the broad category and the specific event(s). In Table 2.1, the specific event was identified as failing grades. It is not unusual, however, to see only the broad category without specified actual stressing event(s). When preparing a multiaxial report, there is no preset limit on the number of psychosocial stressors that can be identified. In general, there is a time limit expected for no more than 1 year prior to the evaluation. Thus, a parental divorce that occurred 2 years prior to the time of the evaluation would not usually be included. There is an exception to the time limit when the event is presumed to continue to be a primary contributor to the present problem condition, for example, in a posttraumatic stress disorder. In earlier versions of the diagnostic manual, the stressor was followed by a numerical assessment of its severity. Some reports will continue to include a numerical or verbal (e.g., mild, moderate, severe) assessment of the estimated severity of the stressing event(s). Giving attention to features in a student's environment that may be contributing to a problem in the school setting is, of course, not new ground for a school counselor. It has been a part of your training from the beginning. Academic problems are sometimes listed on Axis IV as contributors to other problems being experienced by the student, for example, anxiety or depression. Academic problems, however, can also be the primary focus of the needed intervention and can be reported instead

TABLE 2.3 Two Examples of Problems in Reading With Family Discord

	Reading Is Primary Disorder	
Axis I	315.00	Reading disorder
Axis II	V71.09	No evident disorder
Axis III		No apparent contribution
Axis IV		Problems with primary support group-family discord
Axis V	GAF = 65	(current)

	Family Dysfunction Is Primary Treatment Focus	
Axis I	V61.20	Parent-child relational problem
Axis II	V71.09	No evident disorder
Axis III		No apparent contribution
axis iv		educational problems-reading
Axis V	GAF = 65	(current)

on Axis I. For example, consider the situation, illustrated in Table 2.3, in which there are problems with grades in reading and some evidence of family discord. The evaluator is required to make a judgment about which is primary and which is secondary. The top example in Table 2.3 shows the reading disorder identified on Axis I, with family dysfunction identified on Axis IV as a contributing feature. Depending on the examiner's judgment, the situation could be coded in the opposite direction. For example, in the lower example in Table 2.3, the family problem is identified on Axis I, and the problems in school are reported as contributing features on Axis IV.

Because the kinds of things listed on Axis IV are probably second nature to you now, the notation on a report can also provide a tool for you to use in assessing the quality of the report and the faith you may want to have in the other findings. As just one example, consider a referral you have made for a student who is experiencing severe symptoms of anxiety that began approximately 5 months before the referral. The multiaxial diagnosis resulting from the referral is in Table 2.4. You know that the father of the student is active-duty military and, for the past 6 months, has been on remote assignment overseas. The evaluation report could be correct, but the omission of information about the possible Axis IV stressor should signal an

TABLE 2.4 Example of Insufficient Attention to Axis IV

Axis I	300.01	Panic disorder without agoraphobia
Axis II	V71.09	No evident disorder
Axis III		No apparent contribution
Axis IV		None
Axis V	GAF = 50	(current)

immediate yellow flag of caution. If the evaluator is correct and the absence of the parent was not related to the symptoms of anxiety, the narrative in the report should make specific reference to confirm not only that the evaluator was aware of the absence but also the reasons why this was determined to be a noncontributing factor. If no reference to this fact is included, you should probably be extremely cautious with other conclusions in the report.

In the rush often associated with evaluations and their reports, it is unfortunately not rare for conclusions to be made on the basis of test scores alone, with insufficient attention to social contributing factors. When it appears that this may have happened, good advice would be to inform the evaluator of your concern. If the answer you receive is not satisfactory, stronger advice would be to seek another referral source. In the example used in Chapter 1, the phone message from the mental health professional did not include specific reference to Axis IV. This alone would probably not be sufficient reason to question the accuracy. Phone messages are necessarily brief, and it would not be unusual for the person doing the evaluation to assume that you were already aware of environmental contributions. In fact, in the example presented, that would seem highly likely because of the presumption that you were in the best position to meet with the family. Omission in phone conversation may or may not be significant. Omission in the report itself is a litmus test in which you can use your professional expertise to assess the quality of the information you are being provided.

Axis III: Are You Well?

The purpose of an Axis III notation in a multiaxial system is to identify a medical condition that is likely to be having some effect on the problem area(s) identified on Axis I or Axis II. Your training as a school counselor provided a strong foundation for evaluation of the psychosocial stressors coded on Axis IV. Most counselor education programs give insufficient attention to the impact of underlying medical/physical conditions on personal, social, and emotional problems. The potential impact is either ignored or addressed by simply suggesting that you should refer such questions to a physician. It is not surprising, then, that counselors and other nonmedical therapists will often fail to consider medical features that may be crucial for understanding the distress an individual is experiencing.

Certainly, you are not in the position to make a medical diagnosis. Referral of such questions to a physician is the professionally responsible and prudent thing to do (and will also help keep you out of court). Although you are not pretending to have expertise in *what or whether* a condition is present, a strong case can be made for the value in your knowing *what behavioral manifestations are likely* when there is a medical condition.

A multiaxial system does allow the person conducting the evaluation to be very specific, if desired, about the proposed cause. If, for example, the evaluator is certain that a mental disorder is the direct result of a medical condition, there is a specific procedure for reporting that belief on Axis I, for example "Mood Disorder Due to Diabetic Condition." You are more likely, however, to see only the mental disorder coded on Axis I, with any related medical condition listed on Axis III.

It is not unusual to find the word *deferred* for the Axis III or Axis IV designation on a report. This identification can communicate a number of different possibilities, including the following: (a) that more information is needed before a conclusion is drawn about the extent of influence; (b) that the situation is so complex that it requires a more extensive analysis; or (c) that the person preparing the report was unduly cautious, carefully covering tracks when attention hadn't been given to potential influencing condition(s). Regardless of the reason, it is prudent to be cautious, particularly if Axis IV is deferred.

Cases involving multiple mental disorders and complex medication conditions are seldom a part of the expected workload of the school counselor, even though such students are enrolled in public and private school settings. However, other professionals in the school may often turn to you for explanation and recommendation about such cases. Medical conditions can also be relevant in situations that typically are considered completely consistent with the role of the school counselor.

Consider two students who have been referred to you by classroom teachers because of evident test anxiety. You are prepared to assist the students, using an imagery procedure (or some other intervention of your choice). Both could be experiencing symptoms warranting the same description on Axis I. Neither has an evident Axis II condition. Both would warrant identification on Axis IV of an educational problem contributing to the anxiety response. Both could have identical present levels of function on a GAF scale.

So, why bother with the diagnostic codes? You are going to provide the same intervention regardless, even if there were differences evident on Axis II, IV, or V.

Consider further that one of the students has a medical condition, a heart condition called mitral valve prolapse. In multiaxial terminology, this condition would be identified on Axis III and is one that periodically results in physiological symptoms which mimic those of an anxiety disorder.

With that additional information, there is now a difference. You may still be well-advised to use the same intervention with both students. In both cases, the stimulus of a test may result in elevated anxiety. There are, however, at least two important differences. One is in your assessment of whether your intervention was successful. Symptom reduction may be more rapid and more apparent in the student without the contributing medical condition, and the intervention with the student who has this heart condition could be prematurely terminated, judged by you as ineffective.

It is not reasonable for you to assume that the student's physician has already shared the fact of the typical association between the medical condition and the experience of anxiety. Simply knowing that an experience, which "feels like anxiety," may have a different cause could be enough to reduce some self-perpetuation of the symptoms.

It is also not reasonable to expect that you have stored and easily accessed memory of the myriad of medical conditions that might have an impact on a student's behavior. In today's world, there are at least two resources for such information. If you want to invest in a desk reference, an example of a comprehensive and easy-to-use book is the *Merck Manual*, cited in the Appendix. If you enjoy using the computer and have access to the Internet, finding definitions and related conditions is as close as your net browser.

Although they are often (and with some basis) referred to as having roots in a medical model, the codes used in diagnostic manuals represent an attempt to steer a middle course on physical versus psychological or developmental causes of human problems. The intent of diagnostic manuals, as noted earlier, has evolved to providing only a shorthand description for use in communication. It is thus possible to use the descriptions for communication regardless of whether you feel that the student's behavior is a result of a dysfunctional family system or a malfunctioning left temporal lobe.

Axis II:
Are You Always This Way?

We move now from the circumstances that may be contributing features in disorders to the disorders themselves. Axis II in a multiaxial system is used to identify factors that *go beyond the moment* and are likely to be highly resistant to change. You may remember, from your courses on counseling procedures and theories, that there is controversy about whether it is possible to remedy the kinds of conditions identified on this axis. Regardless of whether the underlying condition is possible to modify, the impact of such a condition can be affected with intervention and new learning.

Perhaps a good way to illustrate this begins with noting that Axis II is used to identify two distinct characteristics: personality disorders and mental retardation. If the diagnosis of mental retardation has been appropriately made, the presence of the condition is assumed to be permanent. The impact of the condition is, though, highly variable and contingent on what kinds of intervention for new learning are provided. It is thus possible to concurrently assume a relatively permanent condition and work diligently and successfully

TABLE 2.5 Personality Disorder Clusters

Cluster	Descriptor	Personality Disorders
A	Odd/eccentric	Paranoid, schizoid, schizotypal
B	Erratic/ overdramatic	Antisocial, borderline, histrionic, narcissistic
C	Elevated anxiety	Avoidant, dependent, obsessive-compulsive

to limit the impact of the condition on the person's success and satisfaction in a variety of social, educational, and occupational activities. To carry the metaphor one step further, a condition of mental retardation covers a variety of degrees of severity. In like manner, the appropriate identification of a condition of personality disorder can indicate the probability of mild to severe symptoms, consistent with the disorder.

By definition, a personality disorder is an enduring pattern of behavior or experience that is evident in a variety of settings, tends to be inflexible and highly resistant to change, begins no later than early adulthood, and creates either personal distress or impairment in ability to cope. Table 2.5 identifies three broad categories or clusters of personality disorders, as used in the *DSM*.

These clusters can help to organize the information about personality disorders, but the categories are not mutually exclusive. It is not unusual for the behavior of the same person to justify identification of disorders from more than one of these clusters. Some of the terms used for the disorders may not be especially descriptive. An example is the personality disorder referred to as *schizoid*. Semantically, this might suggest that the person has an extremely severe problem that would warrant immediate hospitalization. In fact, this diagnosis reflects a person who, to an extreme, detaches from social interactions and exhibits a very narrow range of emotions (a loner). Another example is the personality disorder identified in our Chapter 1 example and illustrated in Table 2.1. A borderline personality disorder may suggest that the person almost has a disorder, is on the border. In fact, this is one of the personality disorders that most interferes with the ability to find success and satisfaction in most settings, particularly those that involve interpersonal relationships (also providing the most frustrating and challenging clients for the professional counselor).

Diagnosis of a personality disorder is in essence not a matter of the extent of deviation from a norm, but instead is done by counting the signs of related behavior to see if predetermined criteria are met. The diagnosis of paranoid personality disorder provides a good illustration.

By definition, this disorder is a pattern of elevated suspiciousness to the extent that the motives of others are frequently questioned. We have all probably been in circumstances where such behavior is far from a disorder and in fact is a highly necessary adaptive tool, essential for interpersonal survival. For your behavior to be appropriately identified as a paranoid personality disorder, you would have to meet the criteria of this being typical of your behavior in a variety of settings, not just specific to one or a small number of situations.

Other specific criteria must be met for identification of paranoid personality disorder, including eliminating medical causes for the feelings. It is important to remember that the diagnostic codes are not intended to identify disorders just because a behavior is culturally different. The designation of personality disorder is limited to pervasive, lasting patterns of inappropriate behavior that either impair performance or create distress. Furthermore, they cannot be explained by legal or illegal substance use or by the presence of an Axis I mental disorder. Considering all factors, it is thus highly unlikely that your elevated suspiciousness warranted diagnosis with paranoid personality disorder (although, if you are right now highly suspicious about why I am writing this book, you might want to check the criteria carefully).

It is unusual for personality disorders to be diagnosed during childhood. More often, you will glimpse the beginnings of these disturbances, which will not become fully evident until early adulthood. Still, you will periodically find a child with a personality disorder pattern that has been evident for the required period of at least 1 year and is not typical for a stage of development.

The term *personality trait* in the diagnostic codes is limited to situations in which the pattern of behavior is creating some degree of disturbance. For example, introversion would not be identified as a personality trait, using the diagnostic codes. An avoidant personality trait could be identified if there was evidence that the characteristic pattern was interfering with daily function or creating distress. An avoidant personality disorder could be identified contingent on the extent to which it was both impairing and pervasive. Here is one way to think of this: If your student has been correctly identified as having an avoidant trait, you, although recognizing that the trait would not be evident in all situations, could probably safely bet on it. It would be evident more often than not. If the criteria for avoidant disorder were met, you could not only bet but safely bet a lot.

It is generally recognized that better knowledge of the intervention strategies to mediate the effects of the well learned maladaptive behavior patterns is an important need. You can expect continuing modification in the identification process as more research is completed. We will return to the topic of personality disorders in the chapters which follow.

Axis I:
Is There Anything Wrong With You?

This section of the chapter will provide only a broad overview of the Axis I identification. Axis I categories form the chapters for most of the rest of the book. In general, Axis I is used to report, with the exception of personality disorders and mental retardation, any and all conditions or disorders that appear to warrant intervention. Some conditions are defined and some are not defined as mental disorders, and more than one condition can be identified on Axis I.

Each condition has a corresponding numerical code; and in some instances, the present level of severity is also noted (e.g., mild, moderate, severe). It is also legitimate to identify a condition with a disclaimer of *in full remission, in partial remission,* or *prior history.* The two remission notations are most often used in instances of substance dependence or abuse but can also be used in other conditions. The prior history notation is most often used when there is insufficient evidence of the condition at the time of the evaluation, but the history suggests a condition that is either known or believed to be persistent over time.

The number of possible conditions or disorders that could be identified on Axis I is quite large, including some common and some very rare disorders. In the chapters that follow, the conditions are clustered in general according to a *likelihood of contact* scale. We will begin the series of V codes, Axis I conditions which you are most likely to encounter in the school setting, and then proceed through a variety of the conditions.

A Quick Look Back

If this chapter were to conclude with a test, it would be assumed that, among other things, you are now able (or better able) to

1. Define the intent of multidimensional scaling, using specific examples from a 5-axis system
2. Identify the level of GAF score that typically suggests need for referral
3. Identify a so-called yellow flag in a psychological report, which may indicate a poorly conducted evaluation
4. Discuss the relevance of medical conditions, with specific examples of how this information might be used by the school counselor
5. Differentiate between personality trait and personality disorder, as the terms are typically used in diagnostic codes

3

The V Codes

ALMOST A MENTAL DISORDER

This chapter begins our tour through the various problems and conditions that in diagnostic coding are most often identified as *the problem*. In multiaxial coding systems, this primary problem will usually be noted and identified on Axis I. This chapter is focused on the kinds of problem areas that are most likely to be a part of the school counselor's responsibility. In future chapters, we will continue this pattern of grouping according to the likelihood that you will be seeing such cases, rather than grouping according to common symptoms.

Is It a Problem or a Mental Disorder?

Imagine that you are a secondary school counselor who has just completed several weeks of required meetings with high school juniors about their course schedules for the coming year. Early one morning before first period, one of these students stops by your office and asks if you have a few minutes to talk. You do in fact have a few minutes that morning and invite the student to sit down.

The conversation begins with the student thanking you for the help with the schedule, specifically noting that you really seemed to care about whether the appropriate courses were being chosen. You are appropriately appreciative for the positive reinforcement but are also beginning to wonder what is really going on. Are you about to hear about an accidental pregnancy? Is there about to be a disclosure of sexual abuse? Has there been a gang-related incident involving this student?

You may be relieved (or may be disappointed) when the student instead tells you that the reason for the visit is worry about the possibility of a low grade in an algebra course. The student thought particularly of you when help was needed, because you recently had helped select the precalculus course for the coming semester, a selection which presumed satisfactory performance in the algebra class.

As it turns out, you do have some ideas that could possibly help the student, and you make arrangements for two or three visits with this student. There is need for assistance with study skills and confidence building, two of the many areas for which your training directly provides the necessary intervention skills.

There is no question in your mind that this is a problem that warrants counseling intervention. Some may be surprised, though, that manuals for diagnosis of mental disorders would agree and, in fact, actually have codes designed for just such cases.

The term *mental disorder* implies that the individual is experiencing significant degrees of distress or difficulty in coping with essential functions in daily living. It is likely, however, that many, perhaps most, of the students for whom you provide direct counseling are not experiencing a level of distress or impaired function that would justify identification as a mental disorder. These students do not have a mental disorder but they do need your help.

It would be easy, in fact, to argue that intervention before the distress reached the criteria for classification as a mental disorder would be a powerful preventative tool. Consider, for example, a situation in which you might be seeing an elementary school-age child referred to you for symptoms of anxiety in the classroom. It becomes immediately evident, as you work with this child, that there are some serious communication problems between the child and a parent. If you are able to help reduce the dysfunction in this parent-child relationship, you would have to be at the same time reducing the risk that this dysfunction could grow into an experience of a level of distress that justified a diagnosis of mental disorder.

Certainly, this is not a new concept for a counselor. Many, in fact, believe that the defining feature of counseling is the focus on intervention before problems become mental disorders.

Diagnostic coding systems also acknowledge the importance of such intervention. Axis I in multiaxial systems, in addition to the identification of mental disorders, is used to identify conditions that involve sufficient distress to warrant intervention even when the criteria for identification of a specific disorder are not met. In the *DSM* system, such conditions are identified as V codes.

Working with students whose needs would be defined with the V code could be described as the area for which school counselors are the specialists. The skills needed with such cases can be every bit as demanding as the skills required for intervention with the more severe diagnostic conditions. A case can easily be made that assisting in the restoration of function from a V code condition may often meet a greater societal need than the partial rehabilitation available with some other disorders.

The remainder of this chapter is devoted to exploration of the V code conditions that most likely seem to be encountered in a school setting. The listing is not all-inclusive but is illustrative of diagnosis of such conditions.

Relationship Problems: Parent-Child and Sibling

The common feature in diagnosis of relationship problems is the obvious one, a "messed up" relationship. The focus of intervention may be on the individuals, on the relationship itself, or on both (if you are a family systems advocate, you have probably already answered the question of where you would put the focus).

Remembering the axis model from the previous chapter, if the level of distress or impairment is sufficient to have created a mental disorder in the person, and there is a contributing relationship problem, the mental disorder is identified on Axis I, and the contributing relationship is identified as a psychosocial stressor on Axis IV. With prevention in mind, however, the distress may not have escalated to the level of a mental disorder, and the relationship issues are the focus of your intervention. In that case (the most frequent, it is hoped), the relationship problem is identified on Axis I, to communicate that relationship issues are the reason for and focus of the intervention.

The *DSM* system, for example, includes different numerical codes for various relationship problems, including parent-child, partner, and sibling. When there is not a specific numerical listing for the relationship (for example, teacher-student), there is a code identified with the letters NOS to indicate a problem that is "not otherwise specified."

For example, a diagnosis coded as V61.20 on Axis I tells you that the condition of the child was not serious enough to provide a major source of distress or impaired function but was serious enough to justify some intervention by a professional, and that intervention should be focused on resolving issues in the relationship between parent and child. In the world of third-party payment and managed care, a V code from a mental health professional has actually told you even more. We will get to that later.

Child or Adolescent Antisocial Behavior

Another common V code situation typical in school counseling is when the student is referred for issues related to conduct in the classroom. When, as will often be the case, the referral is the result of an isolated incident rather than a pattern of behavior, the behavior does not warrant diagnosis as a mental disorder. This is an instance in which the use of the alphanumeric code may be far more descriptive than the verbal identification.

Compare the semantic implications of "child antisocial behavior" and "oppositional defiant disorder." The former sounds like a much more serious condition than the latter. In fact, the oppositional defiant disorder condition is a continuing pattern of hostile and disobedient behavior involving authority figures that has persisted for at least 6 months, a much more severe problem than the condition diagnosed as child antisocial behavior. The latter communicates that the misbehavior is serious enough to justify some intervention but has not become a pattern.

Academic Problems

Our first example in this chapter illustrated the diagnosis of an academic problem that was not a mental disorder. There is no intent, though, to suggest that every student with failing grades or marked underachievement should be assigned a diagnostic code (unless, of course, one believes that all such students need counseling). An Axis I diagnosis suggests that there is a condition in which intervention is needed. A V code, in this case, would mean that there was not sufficient evidence to justify identification of one of the conditions defined as a learning disorder.

Phase of Life Problem

What about normal problems faced by normal people in the normal process of growth and development? Phase of life problems are just what the name implies. They are problems that are often associated with developmental stages and warrant professional intervention.

It is important to emphasize that diagnostic coding is not limited to conditions of *abnormality*. When you provide brief counseling intervention for a student having some struggle with developmental tasks associated with early adolescence, the need for this intervention can be documented on Axis I in multiaxial coding (and is often just as significant, just as crucial as that provided by a peer working in a mental health setting with a patient who has a bipolar disorder).

Abuse and the V Code

Throughout this chapter, there has been suggestion that the V codes are typically used to describe conditions that are not sufficiently severe to be defined as mental disorders but are creating enough distress to warrant intervention. To this point, the only exception noted was in the code V71.09, which is usually a way of saying that no intervention is needed.

There is another exception to this general rule of *less severe*. As counselors, we are increasingly asked to provide assistance in situations that involve physical abuse, sexual abuse, or child neglect. There is no question that distress or impairment warranting identification as a mental disorder is most often an outcome for the child or adolescent who has been a victim of such abuse or neglect. Furthermore, a perpetrator of abuse or neglect would seem, by the very act, to have shown evidence of a mental disorder.

When the treatment focus is related to abuse or neglect, there are also special codes that can be used which do not identify the condition as a mental disorder. For example, a V code can be used when the focus of intervention is on the perpetrator of child abuse or when the focus of treatment is on the relationship unit (family system) in which the abuse occurred. Other special codes are available when the focus of intervention is on a child or adult who has been victimized.

Although these special codes are available, they are not used as often as the codes for the disorders created by or associated with the abuse. Table 3.1 illustrates two alternatives for diagnostic coding when the intervention is focused on the perpetrator of abuse.

It is difficult to even conceptualize that a perpetration of abuse could occur in the absence of definable mental disorder, and the primary identification of a mental disorder is the more likely of the two alternatives for the adolescent perpetrator described in Table 3.1. The other choice might be used, however, when there was not sufficient evidence to identify a specific mental disorder. Abuse could also be the primary code used when treating a victim if there was any evident present or future risk to the victim in being identified as having a mental disorder.

TABLE 3.1 Alternative Coding for Adolescent Perpetrator of Abuse

	Mental Disorder Is Primary Code	
Axis I	312.8	Conduct disorder—adolescent onset/severe
Axis II	V71.09	No evident disorder
Axis III		No apparent contribution
Axis IV		Problems with primary support group—sexual abuse; inadequate discipline
Axis V	GAF = 40	(current)
	Abuse Is Primary Code	
Axis I	V61.21	Sexual abuse of child
Axis II	V71.09	No evident disorder
Axis III		No apparent contribution
axis iv		problems with primary support group—inadequate discipline
Axis V	GAF = 40	(current)

Concluding Comment

In this chapter, we have examined a number of conditions that may often be the focus of intervention by a counselor. In some instances, the issues have resulted in an identifiable mental disorder. When that is the case, the disorder would be identified on Axis I in a multiaxial system, and the contributing condition would be noted on Axis IV. It has been emphasized that any one of these conditions, for example a parent-child relation problem, can also legitimately be *the* reason for intervention. In those cases, the appropriate code is noted on Axis I in a multiaxial system.

Before concluding this chapter, it seems important to point out that a V code diagnosis is probably not identified on Axis I as the primary focus of attention nearly as often as actual prevalence would seem to dictate. The flaw, if one chooses to identify it as such, is most likely not so much in the coding system as in the use of it.

Without getting into the sociopolitical issues involved, it seems sufficient to note that most third-party payment for mental health services requires the identification of a mental disorder. When, for example, a parent-child relation problem is identified on Axis I as the primary focus of treatment, there is a high probability that no third-party reimbursement will be available. If the provider can find sufficient evidence to identify another disorder on Axis I, for example, anxiety, and then list the parent-child problem on Axis IV, the probability of eligibility for reimbursement by an insurer increases dramatically.

In fairness, one should at least consider the hypothesis that V codes do not occur as often on reports, because persons who are in a position to receive such reports would more often have condition(s) that justify the code indicating greater distress or severity. That possibility should probably not be discarded without at least some consideration.

With the above acknowledged, until or unless third-party reimbursement becomes available before problems become severe, V codes will probably be reported on Axis I at a lower rate than codes that are eligible for reimbursement. In school counseling applications, at least at this time however, your position is different. In use of diagnostic coding, you have the opportunity to report the V code conditions as they occur, not as they are likely to be reimbursed.

In our next chapter, we begin examination of conditions that are technically defined as mental disorders. The adjustment disorders to be explored in the chapter differ from many of the disorders in that there is an identified *cause* for the symptoms.

A Quick Look Back

It is assumed that, among other things, you are now able (or better able) to

1. Explain the primary use of the V codes, with particular attention to their relevance in the work of the school counselor
2. Identify codes in problem areas often associated with the work of the school counselor

3. Discuss semantic issues related to the V code for childhood antisocial behavior

4. Discuss the use and purpose of the V and corresponding code in instances of childhood abuse or neglect

5. Provide reason(s) for the greater incidence of mental disorder codes over V codes in most intervention settings

4

The Adjustment Codes

A DISORDER FOR EVERYONE

Emphasized throughout this book is the fact that diagnostic coding is primarily used to describe an existing condition, including both medical and psychosocial features that may be contributing to the condition. By avoiding identification of probable cause, the coding system can be generalized to a variety of different intervention models and counseling theories.

The conditions to be described in this chapter are an exception to the rule of "no causative position assumed." Instead, by definition, each of these conditions is identified as an adjustment disorder because in fact there is an assumed cause. When these codes are used, it is assumed that the distress is a result of difficulty in adjusting to something. The codes are then used to identify how the problems in adjustment are being expressed.

When Is Adjustment
a Mental Disorder?

The answer to this question is both simple and complex. In simplest form, an adjustment disorder is a mental disorder when the reaction is greater than would be normally expected from the stressing event or if there is evidence that the reaction is resulting in a severe impairment of function.

On the other hand, when is a mental disorder an adjustment disorder? Again, the answer is both simple and complex. In simple form, an adjustment disorder is coded on Axis I in multiaxial systems when the reaction is sufficiently severe to meet criteria for mental disorder and when there is not sufficient severity to justify coding of another condition.

This can get confusing, so let's go back a bit. Axis I in a multiaxial system is used to identify *the* problem, a condition that is evaluated as sufficiently distressing or impairing to warrant professional intervention. Axis IV in multiaxial coding systems is used to identify psychosocial stressing events that appear to contribute to the presence of the condition.

Second only to the V codes, it is highly likely that students being seen by school counselors for help with personal, emotional, and social problems are those who have problems that would be identified as adjustment disorder. Most children and adolescents are able to adjust to changing circumstances without a serious impairment in function, but some are not.

The term *psychosocial* is used very broadly, including any stressor that is not biological in nature. The student's parents are getting a divorce. The student is attending a new school. The student's parent has a serious physical illness. The student's parent has lost a job. The student is being harassed by gang members.

These and, of course, many more are examples of life events that often create personal distress. If a student with personal, social, or emotional problems is referred to you, it is routine for you to spend time in the counseling session identifying recent events that may be contributing to the distress.

It is not, however, an adjustment disorder yet. Remember that the coding of a disorder comes with the intervention or with an evaluation to identify whether intervention is warranted. If a tree falls in the woods and no one is around, is there a sound? I don't know. But if a person has an intense reaction to a psychosocial stressor, and that reaction never comes to the attention of the counselor, the person, in the strictest sense of the word, does not *have* an adjustment disorder.

This is not intended to convey or assign unbridled power to you (they don't have an adjustment disorder unless *I* say so). It is instead just another reminder that diagnostic coding systems exist to facilitate communication among professionals. *Adjustment disorder* is a term we use to describe and communicate a condition of distress. The coding systems may or may not mirror real life. The value of the coding is not whether it is true in the absolute sense of that term but whether it is an accurate description of a condition, prepared in a form to facilitate communication.

We return to the student who has come to you with a problem. You have identified one or more events in that student's life that would reasonably create some personal distress. It's still not an adjustment disorder. Next, there has to be evidence that the distress level is more than would be expected from the stressor, or evidence that the stressing event has led to significant problems in coping with everyday demands. For situations involving the school counselor, the latter will often be evident in a drop in academic performance or a sudden increase in conduct problems in the classroom.

In actual practice, the impairment criteria for an adjustment disorder is easier to identify than the "more than normal" reaction. When a student who has a history of A and B grades suddenly starts getting Cs and Ds, and upon investigation you learn that the drop in academic performance coincided almost exactly with the separation of the parents, it's not difficult to connect the two events.

Consider instead a student who has been transferred to a new school. The student, who in the prior school had been outgoing and involved in a variety of activities, becomes withdrawn and apparently hesitant to interact with others. We have an event. We have a reaction. The difficulty is in deciding when and whether the reaction exceeds what would be "normal" in such case. Some delay in social interaction in a new school setting would certainly not be abnormal. Determining when normal has been exceeded requires that "normal" has been defined. Easy to say, hard to do.

In actual practice, most who use the diagnostic coding systems will put more emphasis on the impairment criteria. This is probably because defining what is in excess of normal is usually, at best, a judgment call. Placing more emphasis on the impairment may be easier but will not always be sufficient.

For example, when you explore potential stressing life events for the student whose grades just fell off a cliff, you might discover that the timing coincided with the death of a grandparent. The impairment of performance criteria was met. But bereavement is not an adjustment disorder. If the student had been very close to the grandparent, a period during which grades just didn't seem to matter would often be a very normal reaction. As subjective as it may be, some attention to the normality question has to be considered when adjustment disorders are identified in diagnostic coding systems.

Does this really matter? After all, your job is to help a child in need. What difference does it make how the condition is *coded*?

Do you provide the same intervention regardless of the problem? If the answer to that question is yes, then diagnostic coding probably doesn't matter. Do you think accurate and effective communication with other counselors is unimportant? If yes, diagnostic coding probably does not matter.

Granted that the above questions were hardly unbiased in intent, of course you do not provide the same kind of intervention for every problem. There are conditions that warrant differing types of interventions. Accurate diagnostic coding contributes to the identification of such instances and enhances professional communication (and, in some cases, may determine whether you are paid for a service).

For the sake of illustration, let's assume that the student showing the withdrawal behavior in the new school setting has exceeded the normal range for such behavior and that the degree of withdrawal is creating some evident impairment in coping ability. Is it an adjustment disorder now? The answer is no, not yet. More features still have to be considered before making this identification.

So far, we have a psychosocial event (school move), a level of distress related to the event that exceeds the norm, and an impairment in the student's coping with everyday demands, an impairment that appears causally related to the psychosocial stressor. Before this condition would be identified on Axis I as an adjustment disorder, the next step is to rule out other, more serious, disorders.

In this case, the more serious conditions would probably be in the family of anxiety disorders, which we will cover in Chapter 5, or in the family of depression disorders, which will be covered in Chapter 6. It is important to remember that a coding of adjustment disorder is used when there is a condition with sufficient severity to warrant identification as a mental disorder *and* when the distress or impairment does not meet criteria for identification of a more debilitating condition.

Continuing to follow this same case, assume that we have ruled out anxiety and depression disorders (and everything else). Is it now an adjustment disorder? After all we've been through, it may not be thrilling to discover that the answer is still, not yet.

When an adjustment disorder is identified on Axis I, there is a criterion that must be met in regard to time periods. In general, the impairment or distress symptoms must begin within no more than 3 months after the stressing event(s). If this student moved to the new school in September and showed no evidence of elevated distress or impaired performance until the following January, the condition is technically not an adjustment disorder.

Furthermore, if the symptoms persist longer than 6 months after the stressing event, the condition is technically not an adjustment disorder. In this case, if the student moved in September, the symptoms began immediately afterward, and the symptoms were still evident in April, the condition is technically not an adjustment disorder.

The 6-month boundary is a bit tricky, however. Distinction can be made between an acute stressing event and a chronic stressing event. If, for example, the effects of the stressing event are continuous (move to a so-called bad school in a tough neighborhood), then the 6-month limitation will usually be ignored.

Obviously, there are a number of steps in diagnosis of an adjustment disorder. The steps we've been through are illustrated in Table 4.1.

TABLE 4.1 Steps for Identification of Adjustment Disorder

1. Does distress exceed normal reaction?
2. Does distress result in impaired function?
3. Does distress warrant diagnosis of a more serious condition?
4. Did distress begin within 3 months of stressing event?
5. Has it been less than 6 months since the stressing event?

Diagnosis of an adjustment disorder assumes that the answer to Questions 1 through 4 is yes. The answer to Question 5 must also be yes unless the stressing event is expected to have a continuous effect.

For now, let's return to the student in the new school. The distress symptoms exceed normal reaction, and the distress results in impaired function. There was no evidence to support a different diagnosis. The symptoms began within 3 months after the move. We have an adjustment disorder.

That was a long journey but, it is hoped, worth the trip. There are still a few more issues to consider regarding the use of the adjustment disorder identification, but first let's deal with the question of *which* adjustment disorder (it's a much easier process than what we've just been through).

Adjustment Disorder Categories: Which Is It?

When the criteria for adjustment disorder are met, the remainder of the diagnostic coding process is simply to identify the most obvious symptoms of distress. There are five primary choices: anxiety, depressed mood, disturbance of conduct, mixed anxiety and depressed mood, and mixed disturbance of emotions and conduct.

Each of these conditions has a distinct code. Not surprisingly, the mixed conditions are found more often than the symptom-specific conditions because distress often involves a number of concurrent feelings. There is also a code for an *unspecified* category, used when the condition clearly meets the criteria for an adjustment disorder but just doesn't seem to fit well into any of the above categories.

Adjustment Disorders:
Is There Anything Else?

The identification of adjustment disorder typically assumes an identifiable stressing event, with the symptoms lasting no longer than 6 months after the stressor ended. It is, however, not always easy to find the immediate end of the stressing event. A medical condition, for example, could be a chronic source of stress. The stress associated with divorce of parents (i.e., financial problems, dispute between parents) can sometimes continue for an extended period of time. The rule of thumb is to "start the 6-month clock ticking" when it would seem reasonable to assume that the most dramatic effects of a stressing event would be over.

In the world of third-party payment for services and managed care, the 6-month criterion can become much more than just an academic coding exercise. For example, let's take the case of the withdrawing student a little further. The stressor was the move to the new school. The primary symptoms were in a dramatic change of behavior, from being outgoing to being withdrawn. In this instance, there is no reason to assume that the outcome of this stressing event should be chronic. The parents are concerned about the long-range effects of this change and take the child to a mental health professional.

Adjustment disorders, by definition, are mental disorders, so the services are eligible for reimbursement through the parents' medical insurance. For illustration, let's assume that the move came near the beginning of a traditional school year, September 1. The symptoms may have been evident immediately after the move, but it would be very unusual (and usually not very sensible) for the parents to have immediately sought professional assistance when there was no evidence of mood or conduct problems. Through September and October, the parents just hoped the symptoms would disappear as the student became more acclimated to the new school. Then, perhaps, they asked for help from the school counselor, who worked with the student through November.

It became evident to the school counselor that the condition was not responding to the kind of intervention that could be provided, given the constraints of other job responsibilities, so referral was suggested. The parents followed the suggestion, but because of the schedule of the mental health professional and the holiday period, the earliest available appointment was near the middle of January.

Intake and assessment procedures occupied the first two sessions, scheduled at 1-week intervals. The mental health professional was thus ready to begin the treatment intervention during the first week in February.

Although this time frame above was created to make a point, the length of time would not be unusual and in fact would not appear to be unreasonable, given the symptoms. The point to be made, however, is that this time period could easily result in having only four sessions to successfully complete this case if the sessions are to be reimbursed through the parents' medical insurance.

The condition was correctly identified as an adjustment disorder to the stressing event of the move. The move was in September. The 6-month time limit for the effect of the move is through the end of February. The insurer allows a maximum of one session per week, thus the total reimbursable time allows four sessions.

The intent here is not to drift into a philosophical discussion of alleged evils of managed care systems or insurance companies. One could, in fact, easily make a case that, given the anticipated symptom resolution from time alone, and the assistance already provided by the school counselor, the mental health professional should be able to successfully complete work with this student in four sessions. Whether you would personally agree with this assessment depends to a great extent on your own philosophy about counseling and about third-party reimbursement.

Instead, the intent in this illustration is to acknowledge the effect such situations do have on the use of adjustment disorder as the primary diagnosis on Axis I. Specifically, it is to note that when third-party payment is involved, identification of the primary condition as an adjustment disorder may not occur as often as would be warranted by the actual data.

Ethical providers do not *create* more serious disorders when there is no evidence for such disorders. It is, though, easy to see how a counselor, when faced with a situation where there is a near balance between identification of an adjustment disorder with anxiety or identification of one of the anxiety disorders described in the next chapter, would opt for the latter.

There is more involved than just payment to the professional (after all, it's actually the parents' finances that will be most affected). Most counselors were not trained to be comfortable in providing services with an imposed time limit. When there is an opportunity to do so (as is often the situation with identification of adjustment or other disorder), selecting the alternative that provides the most flexibility in delivery of the services is an easily rationalized behavior.

Independent of issues related to reimbursement, it may appear to you that both the 3-month (time for symptoms to begin) and 6-month (time for symptoms to end) periods are a bit arbitrary. If the thought has occurred, you are correct. Both periods are arbitrary, with perhaps some basis in empirical data, but mostly the result of consensus among those who designed the diagnostic coding system.

Remember, though, that the primary intent of coding systems is only to create a shared language for communication. All categorization systems by definition require the drawing of somewhat arbitrary lines. In the case of adjustment disorders, the focus is on the expected onset and termination of symptoms. In other conditions, the focus will be on the number of different symptoms that have to be evident to identify a condition. As is the case with all operational definitions, whether this is or is not a problem with the system lies in the extent to which the definitional lines are clearly drawn and easily communicated.

Before we leave the general category of adjustment disorders, there are three additional things that need to be considered. First, there is one clear exception to the use of adjustment disorder when the conditions came from a stress event. We've already noted that when the distress or impairment warrants identification of a more severe Axis I condition, the latter takes precedent even when there is a direct connection to the stressor.

A special example of this is in the identification of posttraumatic stress disorder. This sometimes controversial identification gained most notoriety in reference to adults who showed later manifestations of symptoms associated with participation in the war in Vietnam. More recently, there has been much discussion regarding the use of this identification for symptoms that appear related to being a childhood victim of sexual abuse. More detailed examination of this disorder is a part of our next chapter.

Still another important consideration related to the diagnostic coding of an adjustment disorder concerns an issue that you may have explored in a methods of research class. That issue is the difference between correlation and causation. We have identified the critical features of an adjustment disorder with the existence of both a stressing event and distress or impairment that came from that event. The best standards of practice would require that alternative hypotheses for explaining the distress or impairment have to be considered before diagnosing an adjustment disorder.

Going back to our example of the student whose withdrawal from social interaction coincided with a move to a new school, the correlation between the two events was clear. In a case such as this, it is very tempting to not bother looking further. It is possible, however, that this could have been a classic example of correlation without causation. Many features in the development of a child can result in a dramatic change in the pattern of social interaction. Up to this point in the example, we have just assumed that the stress of the move elicited the withdrawal behavior. The link should never be assumed, even when it appears to be a logical outcome. Time spent with the student and with the parent, gathering history and exploring other alternatives, is crucial.

Appropriate use of the diagnostic coding systems absolutely requires that there be some sensitivity and knowledge about the student's ethnicity and cultural background. Determining whether a response is more than a normal reaction to a stimulus cannot be done without recognition that definitions of normality in extent of response are not identical across cultures. This is an easy "prescription" for me to write, but the practice of it requires significant skill. Errors can be made in either direction. It certainly would be inappropriate to dismiss a student's concerns because "they" always seem to overreact. It is equally inappropriate to ignore the cultural context in which an individual's response is occurring.

Finally, although this chapter has included continuing reference to the adjustment disorder coding as indicating a condition *less severe* than other mental disorders, this should not be interpreted to mean that the adjustment disorder conditions have no serious consequences. For example, the presence of an adjustment disorder has been shown to be related to increased risk for suicide attempt.

It might be expected that the risk of having an adjustment disorder would be somewhat higher among disadvantaged persons, most likely because of the increased likelihood of having to cope with psychosocial stressors, but adjustment disorders are found across socioeconomic lines. Adjustment disorders appear equally likely for males and females.

Through the course of your workday, you are most likely to be working with students whose condition would be diagnosed with a V code. Students with conditions diagnosed as adjustment disorders probably would be a close second. Consideration of the more serious disorders begins in the next chapter, with the conditions defined as anxiety disorders.

A Quick Look Back

It is assumed that, among other things, you are now able (or better able) to

1. Define the criteria used to identify an adjustment disorder
2. Identify the codes for the six types of adjustment disorders
3. Discuss implications of the time limits in adjustment disorders as these might affect third-party reimbursement
4. Describe the need for caution related to cause-correlation issues and adjustment disorders
5. Discuss the significance of cultural and ethnic features in appropriate coding of adjustment disorder

The Anxiety Codes

A DISORDER FOR ANYONE

The many conditions associated with the term *anxiety* truly would seem to meet the criterion in the title of this chapter. Anxiety is a "disorder for anyone." It is estimated that some 5% to 15% of the population will experience symptoms with sufficient severity to warrant identification as one of the specific anxiety disorders. That may seem like bad news, but there is good news as well. Of the different conditions that can be classified as mental disorders, the anxiety disorders are among those that seem to be most easily relieved with appropriate intervention.

Most of us can easily identify the feelings associated with anxiety. The heart rate is elevated, and perspiration is excessive. Muscles are tense. The mouth is dry. These physiological feelings are often accompanied by rapid and jumbled thoughts, feelings of faintness, feelings of panic: I'm going to die; I have to get away from here; I can't breathe.

The experience of anxiety is a mixed blessing. On the one hand, the feelings associated with anxiety serve an arousal function, which makes it possible to cope with the problems of life. Anxiety about an upcoming test can create the conditions that motivate more study and better performance on the test. The uneasiness in the pit of the stomach before making a presentation can help provide the alertness and drive that facilitate maximum performance.

In a technical sense, the relationship between anxiety and performance can usually be described as curvilinear; too little is bad and too much is bad. The conditions diagnosed as anxiety disorders are those in which the experience is excessive and the anxiety interferes with the capability to cope with the demands of everyday life.

This chapter examines diagnosis of the anxiety disorders often encountered in the school-age population. First, though, it will be helpful to review the underlying physiology of an anxiety response.

What Is an Anxiety Response?

We begin, appropriately enough, with the nervous system itself. You either *are* or *have* a nervous system (a question that we will leave for the philosophers).

The human nervous system divides into two parts: central and peripheral. The central nervous system consists of the brain and the spinal cord. The peripheral is the rest of the nervous system.

The peripheral then divides into two parts: somatic and autonomic. The somatic component of the peripheral nervous system (remember *soma* for body) deals with functions under the direct control of the central nervous system. In the central nervous system, you recognize the need to turn a page in this book. The somatic component of the peripheral nervous system activates the muscles that produce this action.

The other peripheral component is the autonomic system, the major contributor to anxiety disorders. The term *autonomic* is often confused with the word *automatic,* and this is not a serious mistake. The functions of the autonomic system are essentially activated automatically, most with an apparent outcome of protection of the entire biological system.

The same muscles may be activated by either somatic or autonomic functions. When you *wink* your eye at someone, this is a somatic response. In the central nervous system, a decision was made and the somatic functions of the peripheral nervous system activated the muscles to perform the behavior.

The *blinking* of the eyes, however, is too important a response to be trusted to the central nervous system. Periodic eye blinks are essential to the health of the visual system (we could get distracted and forget to blink). Control of the eye-blinking response is an autonomic function. No conscious decision in the central nervous system is required.

Finally, the autonomic component of the peripheral component of the nervous system (this could be a song) divides into two functions as well: sympathetic and parasympathetic. The sympathetic function is the heart of an anxiety response. The parasympathetic function is a significant mechanism for control of anxiety responses.

Excessive anxiety can thus be appropriately described as the outcome of excessive function of the sympathetic component of the nervous system. This physiological link is occasionally evident in the verbiage when elevated anxiety is described as autonomic hyperactivity.

Although the physiological expression is focused in the peripheral nervous system, it would be a mistake to ignore the contribution of the central nervous system in expression of excessive anxiety. Anxiety reactions typically begin in the central nervous system with a stimulus that is interpreted as a threat. Perhaps with a genetic link back to saber-toothed tigers and very large reptiles, a threat perceived in the central nervous system inevitably results in a physiological activation through the peripheral autonomic system. Fight or flee might be a remnant of the only available alternatives when the threat was reptilian.

Fight or flee provides the psychobiological explanation for the feeling that might be experienced when faced with a more contemporary threat. Sometimes, you might feel like running away. Sometimes, you might instead feel that you'd like to punch out the person presenting the threat.

In understanding the anxiety response, it is important to recognize that fight or flee feelings are simply reactions to what the body has been prepared to do. There does not appear to be a genetically programmed reaction for "let's sit down and try to talk this through rationally." Instead, the sympathetic system has activated endocrine secretion from the adrenals, which results in a number of physiological responses, and has redirected blood supply to energize the large muscles.

In essence, the above is *what happens* with the experience of anxiety. As noted at the beginning of this chapter, anxiety is an outcome that can be either a very helpful adaptive mechanism or a mechanism that severely impairs the ability to cope with everyday demands. For the remainder of this chapter, we will explore the diagnosis of conditions when anxiety is at a level that consistently results in such impairment, particularly the anxiety disorders most likely to be encountered in the school-age population.

Generalized Anxiety Disorder

The condition diagnosed as generalized anxiety disorder (GAD) is the logical place to begin. This condition is sometimes referred to as the "flu" of the anxiety conditions. GAD might not result in dramatic impairment in function, but elevated symptoms of anxiety are evident in a variety of different settings. It typically has a gradual onset period and most often begins in childhood or adolescence. At one time, a distinction was made between childhood and adult versions of the disorder, with the former termed *overanxious disorder of childhood* (or adolescence). The GAD designation is now typically used for all age levels.

Consider a student referred to you because of apparent test anxiety. In your session with this student, you discover that taking a test was only one of the situations that resulted in elevated anxiety. The student tells you, "I try to hide it, but I feel worried almost all of the time. It's hard for me to go to sleep at night. I'm sure that I won't do things as well as my parents and teachers think I should. I try not to let people see how scared I am, but sometimes my hands even start to shake."

This student illustrates the classic criteria for diagnosing a generalized anxiety disorder. The symptoms must be almost always present at some level (typically more than half the days over a 6-month period). The symptoms must be evident in more than one setting (test anxiety was only one of the circumstances). The student has difficulty controlling the anxiety. In reference back to the functions of the nervous system, the autonomic sympathetic response may not be extremely elevated but it appears to always or almost always be "on." Performance anxiety is a typical characteristic of GAD.

In diagnosing an anxiety disorder, a number of alternative reasons for the symptoms must first be eliminated. The excessive anxiety cannot be a result of response to a medical condition, a medication, or drug abuse. A direct connection between the symptoms and a particular stressing event (adjustment disorder) must be ruled out.

There are two especially difficult features in diagnosing GAD. One is that the distress must result in *clinically significant* impairment in ability to function. This is often difficult, because many children and adolescents with sufficient symptoms for diagnosis with GAD do in fact find ways to go on about their lives.

One way to determine whether there is a clinically significant impairment is to make a judgment about whether the level of function could be significantly improved if the level of distress were to be significantly reduced. Would the former go up if the latter went down?

The other particularly difficult aspect of diagnosing anxiety disorders is in separating the normal anxiety experiences of everyday life from the levels of anxiety that warrant designation as a mental disorder. One difference is that students with normal levels of anxiety are more likely to feel they have some control over the anxiety. Students with normal levels of distress are also less likely to experience the anxiety on a continuous basis.

Statistics regarding the likelihood of experiencing GAD during one's lifetime will vary according to the source. It is certainly not a

TABLE 5.1 Diagnosing Separation Anxiety Disorder

1. Is the distress at separation more than the norm for the age level?
2. Are there multiple distress symptoms (e.g., refusal to go to school, nightmares with theme of separation, dread in anticipation of possible separation, etc.)?
3. Is the distress persistent (condition lasted longer than 1 month)?
4. Is this a child or an adolescent?
5. Is the distress interfering with ability to function in everyday life?

marked gender difference in this condition, with the ratio of females to male approximately 2:1 in favor of (odd use of the words) the females having GAD.

A GAD diagnosis does not imply opinion about the underlying cause. Some feel that this disorder has roots in unresolved underlying issues. Others emphasize inappropriate conditioned responses. With this condition, the diagnosis confirms the need for intervention. The type of intervention will be selected for other reasons.

Separation Anxiety Disorder

GAD could be described as a "little anxiety everywhere." A separation anxiety disorder is diagnosed when the anxiety symptoms appear to have a specific cause. Separation anxiety can begin as early as the preschool years. It is unusual for the disorder to first appear during adolescence, but it is not unusual for the disorder to continue into adolescence when it began earlier.

The most difficult task in diagnosing a separation anxiety disorder is identifying when the distress is more than a normal reaction. A 3-year-old who cries when left with a baby-sitter would obviously not be automatically diagnosed with this disorder. Course work in human growth and development provides essential information in determining whether a response is more than an age-appropriate reaction. Table 5.1 lists the primary questions for diagnosis of separation anxiety disorder.

Differentiating separation anxiety disorder from generalized anxiety disorder is seldom difficult. In the former, there is a specific event (or perceived event) that triggers the elevated activity of the peripheral sympathetic nervous system function. A student diagnosed with the condition of generalized anxiety may experience severe distress in association with separation issues but will have similar distress with many other stimuli.

It is also relatively easy to differentiate separation anxiety disorder from another diagnostic condition that may produce similar symptoms: the pervasive developmental disorder. This developmental disorder is extremely severe and is often associated with an Axis II identification of mental retardation.

Diagnosing separation anxiety disorder instead of panic disorder is primarily on the basis of what causes the distress. The severity of distress in separation anxiety can be just as intense as in the panic disorder, but the latter is not associated only with concerns about separation. Some cases of panic disorder are identified in childhood but the more typical onset of a panic disorder is late adolescence through the age of "thirtysomething."

The Phobias

You may remember from an introductory psychology course that a phobia is an intense, irrational fear of a specific person, place, or thing. There are two types of phobic conditions: specific and social.

A specific phobia for a child or adolescent has five key features, related to

1. What causes it (must be a person, place, or thing)
2. What happens (inevitable anxiety response)
3. How is it dealt with (avoidance if at all possible)
4. What happens when avoidance is impossible (intense distress)
5. How long has it lasted (at least 6 months)

Children and adolescents may or may not be aware that their fear is excessive. As with all disorders, there must be evidence that the symptoms are not better described by another condition.

Again, as with other mental disorders, the specific phobia must be causing significant difficulty in coping with everyday demands of life. Many of us have unreasonable fears, often coming from a particularly unpleasant situation or from observational learning. In most cases, they don't produce any significant impairment in our ability to cope. A person who has a phobic response to moss on a tree could meet the avoidance criteria easily and not justify a specific phobia diagnosis (especially if living in the desert).

The requirement that the irrational fear must continue for at least half a year recognizes the normality of specific fears in the school-age population. In the normal course of development, there will be specific irrational fears that come and go without warranting diagnosis of a mental disorder.

The criteria for diagnosing social phobias are very similar to those used to diagnose a specific phobia. The difference is that in a social phobia, a social situation is the stimulus that produces the anxiety response. In a social phobia, the situation often involves some expected performance that includes evaluation of that performance (although this may call to mind your feelings about an oral comprehensive examination, remember the other criteria before self-diagnosing).

A common theme of social phobias is the fear of embarrassment. Social phobias can begin during childhood but more often do not occur until the midadolescent years. A social phobia can be generalized (essentially all social situations) or can be associated with only some social situations.

Differentiation between social and specific phobic conditions can be made on the basis of whether the irrational anxiety is elicited by the place (specific phobia) or by what the individual is expected to do in that place (social phobia). For example, consider a lecture auditorium in a typical university setting. If the phobic response occurs only when a speech in front of the class is expected, the identification would be social. If the phobic response occurs *to the place*, regardless of whether one is performing or just sitting, the identification would be specific phobia.

Avoiding situations in which there may be some required social interaction is also found in the diagnosis of another mental disorder: panic disorder with agoraphobia (anxiety associated with feeling or fear of being trapped). Social phobia is the better diagnosis when the distress is associated with whether the social interaction is likely to be evaluated. Another differentiating feature is that having a companion present will usually reduce distress in a panic disorder, but in a social phobia, the companion just adds to the distress (still another person who will be judging the performance).

Posttraumatic Stress Disorder

The diagnosis of posttraumatic stress disorder (PTSD) has received a great deal of attention in the media, not all of it positive. PTSD is often intertwined with some contested societal issues, including antiwar demonstrations and the so-called false memory syndrome. As we examine this condition, it is important to separate the controversial positions regarding cause from the reality of distress that may be a part of the life of the student.

PTSD begins with exposure to an extremely horrific event. The student may have been the victim, may have been a direct observer, or may have just later learned about the event. Examples of the kinds of events that could lead to PTSD include observing a violent death, a robbery, a kidnapping, a serious automobile accident, a natural disaster. Victimization through sexual molestation is included in the listing of events sufficient to trigger PTSD, regardless of whether there was actual or threatened physical danger.

There is a clear relationship between PTSD and the adjustment disorders. In both, the distress is linked to a prior experience. The difference is the severity of the event. A child's distress elicited by the loss of a friend could be either an adjustment disorder or PTSD, contingent on the circumstances that led to the loss (e.g., moving to another part of the city versus death in an automobile accident). Questions for diagnosing PTSD are given in Table 5.2.

For children, the response at the time of the event can include agitated or disorganized behavior as well as the more typical extreme fear or depression responses. The requirement is just that there be some connection between the trauma and the response. When the

TABLE 5.2 Diagnosing Posttraumatic Stress Disorder

1. Was there either direct or indirect experience of a severely traumatic event?
2. Was there some form of severe response when the event occurred?
3. Has there been continuing reexperience of the trauma?
4. Has there been a pattern of avoidance of stimuli that are in any way associated with the event?
5. Have the symptoms been evident for at least 1 month?

distress symptoms were already evident before the trauma, the event may be exacerbating the distress, but this is not diagnosed as PTSD.

There is one exception to the requirement that there be evidence of serious distress at the time the event occurred. Developmentally inappropriate sexual experience may or may not result in an immediate distress response. In the case of sexual abuse, the event alone is interpreted as evidence of severe response to the experience of a traumatic event.

For adults, the connection between the trauma and the experience is usually explicit. In children, the trauma may be experienced in a generalization of extreme distress, sometimes in nightmares without clear content connection.

Reexperience of the distress associated with the trauma can take many forms, most of which are associated with the peripheral sympathetic nervous system functions. Difficulties in maintaining concentration, sleep difficulties, and an elevated startle response are examples of these symptoms.

Some with PTSD experience extreme feelings of detachment from others. Some have a severely restricted range of emotions. Avoidance of associations with the trauma can also take many forms, one of which is simply the loss of memory associated with that time period.

A diagnosis of PTSD on Axis I in a multiaxial system requires additional descriptive information. PTSD should be identified as either acute or chronic, depending on whether the symptoms have lasted more or less than 3 months. The condition should be identified as delayed onset if the impairing symptoms did not begin until 6 months or more after the traumatic experience.

PTSD is an example of a condition in which making the appropriate diagnosis is a crucial factor in providing the most appropriate intervention. For example, think about a child who seems to be having very severe anxiety symptoms associated with the school setting and, in response, just refuses to go to school.

There are a number of possible intervention strategies for such a situation, and the selection of the most appropriate may be contingent on an accurate diagnosis. As one example, refusing to go to school could be the result of a conduct disorder, which might respond quickly to an intervention strategy based on contingencies of behavioral reinforcement. If the behavior instead is reflecting PTSD, that strategy is unlikely to be helpful and could very well be counterproductive.

The next chapter continues our consideration of the more severe disorders with examination of the various disorders of depression. Although in separate chapters in this book, symptoms of anxiety and symptoms of depression are often concurrent. Anxiety symptoms are often so visible that they can temporarily hide a depressive disorder.

A Quick Look Back

A test on this chapter would assume that you now have increased capability to

1. Describe the physiological basis for the experience of anxiety
2. Differentiate among conditions of normal anxiety, adjustment disorders with anxiety, and anxiety disorders
3. Explain how the generalized anxiety disorder condition differs from more specific anxiety conditions, including separation anxiety
4. Differentiate between the conditions of specific phobias and social phobias
5. Explain the distinction between posttraumatic stress disorder and the adjustment disorders that also assume an eliciting event

6

The Depression Codes

WHEN SADNESS BECOMES A DISORDER

Childhood is an idyllic period, characterized by supportive family gatherings, picnics on beautiful spring days, playing games with friends. Childhood is a period of ongoing trauma, characterized by gloom and despair, harsh punishments, embarrassment, feeling unwanted and unloved.

Which is it? For a fortunate few, the idyllic description may be true. For an unfortunately large number of children, the despair and fear are clearly predominant. The answer for most is that childhood is a mixture of both these extremes, feeling cared for and feeling abandoned, feeling safe and feeling at risk.

This chapter is about the bleak side of childhood and adolescence. Suicide ranks high among causes of death among children and adolescents. Even when there is no elevated suicide risk, a school

counselor will not soon forget the sad eyes and flat affect of a child
who is experiencing major depression.

Major Depressive Disorder

There are many symptoms associated with depression. These
include extreme fatigue or excessive agitation, low self-esteem, sleep
disorders, extreme difficulties in concentration, and continuing
thoughts of suicide. Significant unintentional weight loss or gain
may signal a depressive condition. In children, a failure to make
age-appropriate gains in weight can be a sign of clinical depression.

A child or adolescent with a depressive disorder might express the
condition with excessive emotional sensitivity. The child or adolescent might be extremely negativistic, or pessimistic. Withdrawal
from social activities and apathy are additional indicators that might
signal the presence of a depressive disorder.

Mary is an eighth-grade student who was referred to you because
of her responses on a self-report questionnaire administered as
part of a group guidance activity. On this questionnaire, she reported a level of distress significantly higher than the norms for
her peer group, including an answer that she often thought about
hurting herself on purpose.

In the course of the interview, she tells you that she has been
feeling extremely "down" for the past 2 weeks and just can't seem
to shake off the feeling. Normally a good student, she has failed
several exams during this period. She tells you that since the
feelings began, they have been with her throughout almost every
day. When asked to be more specific about the feelings, she tells
you that she is tired all the time even though she has been going
to sleep early and sleeping late. She tells you that she is finding it
almost impossible to pay attention in her classes. She tells you that
she has no specific plan for an attempt but finds herself often
thinking about suicide. It is evident both in her words and in your
observation that she has lost interest in activities that had been a

TABLE 6.1 Major Mood Disorders in Children and Adolescents

Diagnosis	Primary Criteria
Major depressive disorder	Major depressive episode
Bipolar I disorder	Major depressive episode plus manic or mixed episode
Bipolar II disorder	Major depressive episode plus hypomanic episode
Dysthymic disorder	Less severe but more persistent symptoms of depressed mood
Depressive disorder NOS	Symptoms of depression that warrant intervention but do not meet criteria for identification of other disorder

source of pleasure for her. Her affect is flat. It appears that she just doesn't care any more.

The situation above illustrates a *major depressive episode*. Specifically, for a period of at least 2 weeks, throughout almost every day, she has experienced symptoms from at least five categories of depression. One of the symptom categories has to be either extreme sadness (which in a child or adolescent can be expressed as irritability in mood) or *anhedonia*, which simply means an apparent lack of ability to experience pleasure. The symptoms must result in some clear impairment in her ability to function. Mary's situation clearly meets these criteria.

Unless a better explanation can be found, the experience of even one major depressive episode is sufficient for diagnosis of major depressive disorder (clinical depression).

Table 6.1 lists the primary mood disorders found in children and adolescents. The diagnosis of major depressive disorder is a significant identification, with important implications for intervention.

The symptoms reported by Mary appear to meet the criteria for diagnosis of major depression, but diagnostic coding of this disorder requires that other possible explanations must be considered and eliminated to confirm this diagnosis. It is particularly important to consider the possibility that the symptoms could be coming either from a medical condition or from the medication being used to treat a medical disorder. Asthma, diabetes, hepatitis, and malnutrition are just a few of the medical disease conditions that can produce symptoms of depression.

Even in situations where a medical condition is not causing the symptoms of depression, there are instances in which a medication being used to treat such a condition has side effects of depression. Examples include some antianxiety medications, hormones, and birth control pills. Although the medications associated with symptoms of depression are more likely to be prescribed to adults, it is crucial to first obtain a detailed and accurate medical history before diagnosing Mary with a major depressive disorder.

Anxiety disorders sometimes mask the concurrent experience of a disorder of depression. Successful treatment of the anxiety can appear to make the individual's overall condition worsen as the symptoms of depression emerge. It may seem that the intervention for anxiety *caused* the depression when in fact the intervention might have only removed the symptoms that were masking it.

Assuming that medical conditions or treatment have been eliminated as the cause for the depressive episode, a detailed psychosocial history is also a critical feature in the diagnostic process. Of particular concern is the possibility that these symptoms are not the result of unsuccessful attempts to adjust to a major stressing event. Mary reported that she had been experiencing the symptoms of depression for 2 weeks. What, if anything, happened in her life immediately before the symptoms began?

Any number of events could have created these symptoms in a person in the early stages of adolescence. Was there a recent breakup with a boyfriend? Did she just learn that her parents were considering separation? Was there a particularly traumatic event associated with biological changes in early adolescence?

If any one of these or many other possibilities was the trigger for the symptoms, the experience can still be extremely devastating, but the diagnosis is adjustment disorder, not major depressive disorder. This distinction is more than just an academic exercise. The modality for intervention and the level of assistance required can be far different for these two conditions.

There is still another feature that must be considered before identification of a major depressive disorder. Mary is an adolescent. Adolescents are unfortunately often at risk for illegal substance abuse. If the substance use/abuse provides explanation for the major depressive episode, the condition is not diagnosed as a major depressive disorder.

Mary's history is obviously a crucial feature in accurate identification of a disorder of depression. Self-report questionnaires can be extremely helpful in identifying children and adolescents who are at risk for depressive disorder and who are reporting systems consistent with such disorder. But *how often?* and *for how long?* become critical questions for appropriate diagnostic coding.

Especially in the gathering of information for the psychosocial history, a school counselor could have a vitally important role in the diagnostic process. Even though you might not be charged with the task of being the diagnostician, you could often be in a position where the student's trust in you results in your receiving crucial elements of information. Given the necessary permission for release of information, that information could be invaluable in accurate diagnostic coding.

We will assume, for illustration, that other explanations for Mary's depressive episode have been eliminated (ruled out). No stressing events appeared to be associated with the beginning of the symptoms. She is taking no prescribed medications, she has no known medical condition that would result in symptoms of depression, and there is no evidence of illegal substance use or abuse.

With the other possibilities eliminated, the experience of just one major depressive episode is sufficient for the diagnosis of major depressive disorder. Coding systems are then used to elaborate the diagnosis with information both about whether this was a single episode or is a recurring condition and about the severity of the symptoms at the time of the diagnosis. For example, in the *DSM* system, Mary could be assigned a code of 296.23 to communicate that this was a single episode of major depression with severe symptoms but no apparent loss in contact with reality.

Mary's condition meets the criteria for diagnosis of major depressive disorder. However, before she is given this diagnosis, there is another disorder to be considered: a bipolar (manic-depressive) disorder.

Bipolar Disorders

Actually, there are two bipolar conditions (bipolar I and bipolar II) that could be consistent with Mary's condition, given the information we have thus far. The experience of a major depressive *episode* was the critical feature in the diagnosis of major depressive disorder. The experience of either a manic or hypomanic episode is the critical feature in diagnosis of the bipolar disorders.

A manic episode is a period of mood disturbance involving symptoms such as excessive talking, distractibility, high-risk behaviors, inflated self-esteem, and sleeplessness that has lasted at least 1 week. Such episodes may require hospitalization and often result in significant impairment in ability to cope with everyday demands.

Determining whether Mary has experienced a manic episode is likely to involve more than just an interview with her. These episodes are often not acknowledged by the person who had the experience but are easily identified by family and friends.

If Mary, in addition to the major depressive episode, has also experienced a manic or mixed episode (alternates between major depressive episode and manic episode nearly every day for at least 1 week), she will have met the criteria for diagnosis of a bipolar I disorder. Bipolar I disorders take precedence in diagnostic coding systems, so in a multiaxial system her Axis I condition will be coded as bipolar I.

Assuming that we found no history of manic episodes in this young adolescent's history, we have just one more thing to consider. A bipolar II disorder is characterized by a combination of major depressive episode and hypomanic episode. This can be a tricky determination.

A hypomanic episode could be defined as "manic lite." The symptoms are essentially the same. There is a shorter duration requirement, 4 days instead of 1 week. Hypomanic episodes do not have psychotic features (manic episodes sometimes do) and hypomanic episodes do not result in as much impairment in ability to function. In fact, in adults, periods of hypomanic episodes have sometimes been associated with temporary dramatic increases in efficiency, productivity, and creativity.

A hypomanic episode is often unrecognized by the individual and is instead interpreted as just temporary relief from the symptoms of depression. The critical question to ask is whether there have been periods when there was extreme difficulty sleeping at night with no corresponding fatigue during the next day.

Numerical coding systems for major depressive and bipolar disorders are complex and unlikely to warrant memorization unless such disorders are a frequent component of practice. Differential diagnosis can be difficult because of the importance and the significance of an accurate history. An in-depth knowledge of human growth and development characteristics is essential to differentiate the characteristics of manic or hypomanic episodes from the normal mood swings of adolescence. The steps in diagnosis among the major disorders, however, are quite straightforward, as illustrated in Table 6.1.

First, there must be evidence of a major depressive episode without other explanation. Then, separation of a major depressive disorder from the bipolar disorders is just a matter of determining whether there have also been manic or hypomanic episodes in addition to the episode(s) of major depression.

Diagnostic coding also allows for some additional nuances or variations. For example, both the bipolar I and the bipolar II conditions can include a specifier of rapid cycling. The *rapid* in such case is a cycling of four or more clearly defined depressive and manic or hypomanic episodes during the period of 1 year.

Cyclothymic disorder is a condition closely related to the bipolar disorders. This condition is characterized by rapidly changing moods with hypomanic episodes and depressive symptoms that do not meet the criteria for major depression. Cyclothymic disorder typically begins during adolescence, and statistics suggest that there can be a near 50-50 risk of later development of the bipolar I or bipolar II condition.

Later in this chapter, we will explore some of the treatment implications for the diagnostic coding of major depression and the bipolar disorders. For now, we found no evidence of manic or hypomanic episodes in Mary's history. Her diagnosis is major depressive disorder.

Dysthymic Disorder

Your next appointment for the day is with another early adolescent. This student also is reported to be experiencing severe symptoms of depression (you're having a tough day).

Lynn is a 13-year-old male who, like Mary, was referred to you as a result of responses on a self-report questionnaire. Lynn also tells you that he is feeling fatigued and listless despite going to bed early and sleeping late. He is feeling very down and has little hope that things will get better in the future. Different from Mary, however, he tells you that he has felt this way for at least 1 year, but not every day. More questioning suggests, though, that over the course of the past year, there have been more "down days" than not, and there was never a period of more than 1 month without the feelings of sadness and depression.

As with all diagnostic coding, it is necessary to determine if these symptoms have caused any significant difficulty in his ability to meet everyday demands. And it is essential that other explanations, including adjustment to a stressor and effects of a medical condition, are eliminated. When the other possible explanations have been ruled out, Lynn meets the classic criteria for diagnostic coding of a dysthymic disorder, a condition once referred to as depressive neurosis.

Dysthymic disorders often begin in childhood or adolescence. In the school-age population, the symptoms typically result in problems in academic performance and in social interactions. The likelihood of a child or adolescent having the dysthymic disorder is higher if either of the parents has been diagnosed with major depressive disorder. Studies have also suggested that approximately 10% of persons with dysthymic disorder will meet the criteria for major depressive disorder during the following year.

When a dysthymic condition precedes a major depressive disorder, both conditions are coded on Axis I in a multiaxial system. This situation is called a double depression.

There is some controversy about whether the condition identified as dysthymic disorder on Axis I in a multiaxial system would be better described as an Axis II personality disorder. Personality disorders are characterized by persistence of the behavior patterns over long periods of time, patterns that are very resistant to modification. Those features are also characteristic of a dysthymic disorder.

Depressive Disorder NOS

The depressive disorder NOS condition is increasingly evident in diagnostic coding. An NOS (not otherwise specified) designation can be attached to almost all the diagnostic conditions. It is, in effect, a "miscellaneous" category and is used, typically with additional explanation, to identify conditions that just don't quite fit the available options but clearly indicate conditions that warrant intervention.

Depressive disorder NOS is intended for use when a disorder involving depression does not meet the criteria for major depressive disorder, dysthymic disorder, or one of the adjustment disorders. It can be used when there are not quite enough symptoms for the other depressive disorder condition, or when there are sufficient symptoms but the duration of the symptoms does not meet the required criteria.

For example, the identification of a major depressive disorder requires that there be a major depressive episode period of at least 2 weeks in which there has been evidence of a variety of symptoms of depression. If Mary, our first example, had serious symptoms for the required 2-week period but only a few different kinds of symptoms, her diagnosis would have been depressive disorder NOS rather than major depressive disorder. If many kinds of symptoms of depression had been evident but only for a short period of time, the NOS condition would be diagnosed.

The primary intent of the NOS designation for the various disorders was in recognition that diagnostic coding systems remain in an imperfect state. The ultimate goal of a coding system is to be all-inclusive, but there is incredible variability in the human condition. The goal is far from being attained with the available codes.

An apparent increasing use of the depressive disorder NOS identification most likely is not the result of an epidemic of this disorder. Because of issues related to third-party payment for services, when an alternative diagnosis is available, there is less inclination to identify an adjustment disorder. Depressive disorder NOS often provides just such an alternative. Although the NOS designation was intended to be used only when criteria for other depression disorders were not met (including adjustment disorders), situations in which there is a close call are probably now often identified with that designation.

Suicide Risk Indicators

Suicide has been ranked as the third-leading cause of death among persons between ages 15 and 24 and the sixth leading cause of death among children between ages 5 and 14. Among the risk factors for suicide attempt are major family conflict, abuse (physical, emotional, or sexual), substance abuse, previous suicide attempts, a family history of suicide, a friend committing suicide, recurrent self-destructive thoughts or behavior, serious medical illness, and availability of guns in the home. Although some of these risk factors are not equally distributed among socioeconomic ranks, any child or adolescent could become suicidal, regardless of gender, ethnicity, socioeconomic class, or age.

Consideration of suicide risk is included in this chapter because of the overlap between some symptoms of mood disorders and increased risk of self-destructive behavior. At one end of the scale, the impulsivity and poor judgment associated with a bipolar manic episode significantly increase the risk of intentional or inadvertent self-destructive behavior. At the other end of the scale, elevated feelings of helplessness and hopelessness are often associated with each of the depressive disorders.

Some have suggested that the feeling of hopelessness is at the heart of essentially all purposeful suicidal acts. This feeling can make a child or adolescent especially vulnerable. Adults who experience periods of feeling "what I do doesn't matter" most often can balance those feelings with memories of comparable periods that were followed by periods with evidence that there was reason for hope. The school-age population, especially children, might not have the balancing experience.

When diagnosing, screening for, or both diagnosing and screening for disorders of depression, it is common practice to include one or more self-report questionnaires. Normative data for these self-reports of distress can be particularly helpful in determining whether the symptoms are outside the norm for a particular age level or gender. Most such questionnaires include at least one question associated with suicide (often phrased as "hurting self on purpose" in questionnaires for younger groups).

When a student responds to an item on a questionnaire in a manner indicating that there has been some thought about suicide, this of course does not mean that there is grave risk that warrants immediate hospitalization. In fact, an adolescent who reports that the thought has never occurred is often an adolescent who does not feel comfortable enough to report the truth on the questionnaire. However, any time such response occurs, the best standard of professional practice mandates that you follow up with some discussion with the student. The probability is that there is no present elevated suicide risk, but the stakes are of course too high to risk being wrong.

Intervention and School Counseling

The bipolar disorders were among the first conditions labeled as mental disorders for which a rather clear biological link was identified and for which a particular medication frequently provided dramatic symptom relief. Obviously, when you suspect that a child or adolescent may meet the criteria for identification of bipolar disorder, an immediate referral is needed.

At the time of this writing, there remains a great deal of controversy about whether the clinical depression condition is best treated with behavior therapy, cognitive therapy, other brief therapies, long-term therapy, medication, or some combination. Advocates for each position can find some support in the research literature. There is clear consensus that if you see a child or adolescent who appears to meet the criteria for identification of major depressive episode, there is sufficient basis for referral for additional evaluation and possible intervention.

Children and adolescents with dysthymic disorder do not typically exhibit the severe vegetative symptoms associated with a major depression. In some ways, however, their needs may be even greater. Persons with a major depression disorder often do find relief and remission of symptoms in medication or therapy or both. The prognosis for success in treating a dysthymic condition is mixed, at best.

Because, however, it is likely that at least some of the dysthymic conditions found in children and adolescents are based on learned patterns of behavior, early intervention seems crucial. By creating school environments that reduce the feelings of hopelessness, supplemented at times with individual counseling sessions, the school counselor may be in a position to have a major impact on reducing the extent and the severity of the dysthymic condition.

The stakes in the differential diagnosis of mood disorders can be high. With the success of the new generation of antidepressant medications, many if not most mental health professionals now recommend the use of psychotropic medications as a part of intervention with severe symptoms of depression. The type of medication used and the predicted results can vary according to the diagnostic code. Selection of the wrong medication might not make the situation worse, but there is also harm in extending the period of discomfort.

Evaluating the need for medication is of course not within the province of the school counselor, and second-guessing the prescribing physician is a behavior unlikely to bring joy into your professional life. However, it is not unusual for either a parent or a teacher to ask your opinion about the expected effects of certain medications. You may philosophically disagree with the conceptualization that you should be a resource of mental health information in the school setting; but, disagree or not, this is still another role often associated with your job.

When the questioner is a parent, the appropriate response is a little easier to identify. Parents should be directed to address any questions to the physician who prescribed the medication. But, before you get too comfortable with this answer, remember that most antidepressant medications are prescribed by general practitioners, not by psychiatrists. It would not be at all unusual for the physician, if asked a question about impact of the medication on school performance, to refer the parent to you for information about school-related outcomes.

In our next chapter, we make a dramatic shift. Thus far, our focus has been primarily in the affective domain. We will next examine the features for diagnosis of learning disorders in the cognitive domain.

A Quick Look Back

If a test were given on this chapter, you would be expected to be able (or better able) to

1. Identify symptoms common to all depressive disorders
2. Describe the relationship between major depressive episode and major depressive disorder
3. Differentiate between bipolar I and bipolar II disorders
4. Take and defend a position on whether dysthymic disorder is best conceptualized as a personality disorder
5. Discuss the features of depressive disorders that are associated with increased suicide risk

The Cognitive Codes

PROBLEM LEARNING OR LEARNING DISORDER

Children and adolescents have academic problems for a variety of reasons, which can be associated with the diagnostic codes. An anxiety disorder can make it almost impossible to pay attention to the teacher's directions. A depressive disorder can make a child or adolescent simply not care what the teacher is saying. Dysfunctional family systems result in some students using poor academic performance as a tool against the parents.

A diagnosis of mental disorder generally requires some evidence of significant impairment in the person's ability to cope with everyday demands. For the school-age population, the impaired function will most often be in the classroom. Mental disorders create problem learners (poor teachers also create problem learners, but that's another story).

Problems in learning can, however, also occur in classes taught by excellent instructors and in students where there is no evidence of the kinds of mental disorders we have described thus far. Learning is, after all, an activity of the nervous system. There is no more basis in assuming that all nervous systems function with equal effectiveness than there would be to assume that any of the other biological systems are equally effective in all students.

School psychologists will, of course, typically have the primary responsibility for diagnosis of the learning disorders. Their specialized training is used to assess the nuances within and among the various conditions associated with the disorders of learning. School counselors are, however, often expected to be able to interpret and communicate results of these specialized evaluations. In this chapter, we will focus on some of the broad concepts essential in evaluation of learning disorders, including some implications for identification of appropriate counseling interventions.

The Language of the School and the Language of Diagnosis

Terminology can become especially crucial in this area because of the implications for special funding or other forms of special educational assistance. The philosophy of inclusion suggests that most students with a learning disorder will be in a regular classroom. The philosophy of individualization suggests that special services are or should be available to all students who have special needs.

You are no doubt familiar with the political and societal debate regarding the extent to which schools are responsible for meeting the special needs of students with disabilities. What to call these conditions is a source of continuing controversy. They have been variously labeled, among other things, disorders, disabilities, impairments, and challenges.

The terminology is often mixed. For example a learning *disability* is defined as a *disorder* in one or more of the basic psychological processes involved in understanding or using language. Consider

Jesse, a student in the fifth grade, who is unable to read a textbook designed for use in a second-grade classroom. Putting all the terms together, Jesse's impairment in reading is a disorder, which is classified as a learning disability that results in Jesse's being *reading-challenged*.

We have a problem with terminology. Jesse's problem is simpler to define. He just can't read.

There is no chance that the terminology issues could be settled in this chapter. The terminology is and will continue to be driven primarily by the ever-changing funding opportunities. Underneath the semantics, though, there are some fundamental and important issues and concerns. Some children and adolescents, despite the best teaching and without other mental disorders, do not experience success in the area of primary responsibility of the schools.

At its essence, the mind is simply what the brain does. For some students who you are asked to serve, the brain isn't doing very well with some tasks.

The Quantified Standard

In the majority of the other conditions identified as mental disorders, the primary source of information for diagnosis is based on direct observation and a history of past observation, usually by parents and teachers. Questionnaires may be used as part of the information-gathering process but do not provide the primary data. When diagnosing learning disorders, results on standardized tests become paramount. Observational information can be used to better interpret the scores on the tests, but the scores themselves are used to provide the essential diagnostic criteria.

The three primary categories of learning disorders are disorders of reading, disorders of mathematics, and disorders of written expression. The common feature is that the performance is substantially below what would be expected from the individual's education, age, and measured intelligence.

When diagnosing learning disorders, an extreme degree of weight is given to the accuracy of the measurement of intelligence. Only when this measurement is reasonably precise will it be possible to provide an appropriate diagnosis.

Consider two students, Shirley and Patricia. Shirley is a very poor reader. Patricia is also a very poor reader. They are the same age and appear to have had the same educational opportunities. It would seem reasonable that each could be diagnosed with a reading disorder. If Patricia also has a poor score on a test of intelligence, she, by definition, would not meet the criteria for identification with the disorder. Both students could be identified as having a learning problem in reading. Only Shirley could be diagnosed with a reading disorder.

Determining which learning disorder is not difficult. Determining whether there in fact is a learning disorder can be very difficult. The complicating feature in this diagnosis is the determination of what would be a reasonable expectation for academic performance. To make this determination appropriately, a brief review of the nature of standardized tests may be essential. To simplify this review, the term *intelligence* will be used as a synonym for tests variously labeled as ability, aptitude, scholastic aptitude, and so forth.

Tests: Looking Under the Hood

Is the level of achievement significantly lower than what would be expected, given the level of intelligence? An answer to this question requires that there be both a measurement of the student's intelligence and a separate and distinct measurement of achievement.

This may not be as easy as it appears. The title on the front page of the test may or may not be an accurate reflection of what is inside. With some limitations for professional respectability, tests are named with a primary goal: sales of the test. It becomes the user's responsibility to have sufficient training to appropriately interpret the results. Problems in the naming of tests have been sufficient over the years to even create a catchphrase: the jingle-jangle fallacy.

Two tests are said to "jingle" when they have similar titles but actually are measuring different things. Tests "jangle" when they have different titles but actually are measuring quite similar abilities.

There are many tests whose titles suggest that they provide the results that could be used to determine what level of performance could be expected. Some of them jingle.

To diagnose a learning disorder, at least two tests would be required: one to assess potential, the other to test actual performance. Some tests, whose titles suggest they could be used to provide such comparison, should not be used in this fashion. They jangle.

A good example of jangling is found in the results from the standardized norm-referenced tests probably administered to all students at various grade levels in your school system. This is often referred to as the sweep testing program.

It is typical for the test battery to include not only measures of achievement but also an additional measure, labeled a test of aptitude or ability. Combining the ability (intelligence) and the achievement measurement into a single battery is touted as a way to determine if the achievement is at a level predicted by the potential.

Look closely at these tests. In the section used to measure achievement in reading, there is usually a vocabulary subtest, most often made up of items requiring the student to select a synonym. In the ability test, you are likely to find vocabulary items that require the student to (guess what?) select a synonym. This is the jangle fallacy. From what appear to be very comparable items, the student will receive a score identified as reading achievement in vocabulary and another score often labeled verbal aptitude. Differences in these scores can be caused by a number of things, including the reliability of the tests or a variation in motivation while taking the test. But these tests cannot be used to identify a learning disorder. They jangle.

The identification of the intelligence level to serve as a baseline for comparison to the achievement test results requires the individual administration of a standard intelligence test. Group intelligence tests (by whatever name) cannot be used to determine this baseline. The group intelligence tests often have significant content overlap with the achievement tests (and of course do not provide control for test-taking motivation).

You may need to be prepared with an answer when a parent asks you about the child's performance on the schoolwide testing program, especially if there was a discrepancy between the aptitude and achievement test scores. The parent may well have read an article in the newspaper or watched a television news show that described special services available for students with learning disorders. The computerized test report received from the school could make it appear that the child has met the criteria for such diagnosis. It could fall on you to explain why the test scores reported by the school did not provide evidence of eligibility for those services.

The Influence of Sensory Deficits

There might seem to be an easy solution to the possibility of overlapping content between achievement and ability tests. That would be to require that the assessment of intelligence come only from use of one of the major tests (e.g., Stanford-Binet, Wechsler Intelligence Scale for Children, Kaufman Assessment Battery for Children). These tests are individually administered and are generally recognized as the primary tools for assessment of intelligence.

However, only about one half of the Wechsler scales can be appropriately administered to students with impaired vision. Comparable difficulties in administration are evident with the other widely used tests, and also for students who have hearing impairment.

When diagnosing a learning disorder in a student with sensory deficit(s), any difficulties in learning must be more than what might be typically encountered in the school setting by that student simply as a result of the sensory issues. The person responsible for gathering the intelligence and achievement data for the student with sensory deficit(s) must be especially sensitive to the special needs of such students. If the intelligence level is underestimated, a learning disorder may go unrecognized. Simply using the so-called standard instruments will not suffice.

The Influence of Cultural Features

The controversy surrounding measurement of intelligence among various cultural groups is well known (and, to some extent, well

TABLE 7.1 Example of Problem in Diagnosing Learning Disorder

| | Wechsler IQ Scores | | | |
Student	Verbal	Performance	Full-Scale	Achievement Test
Jeff	75	125	100	Low
Rob	100	100	100	Low

founded). Remember that the essence of diagnosis of learning disorder is a substantial difference between the student's capability and the student's performance. Just as was the case with the sensory deficit, if the intelligence level is underestimated, misdiagnosis or lack of diagnosis of learning disorder becomes likely. Again, limiting measurement of intelligence to the standard instruments may not be sufficient.

Consider the two students described in Table 7.1. Both have poor levels of achievement. Is there a learning disorder?

Both Jeff and Rob have full-scale IQ scores of 100. Jeff, however, has a very low score on the verbal section but a compensating high score on the performance section. Rob's performance was consistent throughout the test.

Beginning with Jeff, here are some of the possibilities. Using the full-scale IQ score as the baseline, unless his achievement test score is extremely low, the criteria for diagnosis of a learning disorder will not be met (the criterion is typically a difference of at least two standard deviations between intelligence and achievement scores). But, suppose that English is a second language for Jeff. In that case, his actual potential would possibly be underestimated by the verbal score, and the performance score instead would be the better baseline measure. The performance IQ score was quite high, so in that case Jeff would most likely meet the criteria for diagnosis of a learning disorder.

Although Rob's intelligence test scores were all at the norm, there is possibility of misinterpretation here as well. As it stands, he probably would not be diagnosed with learning disorder. What if English were also his second language? In that case, the "normal" level of verbal IQ score could for him be an underestimate as well. He could, in fact, have very high intelligence and thus meet the intelligence-achievement discrepancy criteria for diagnosis of learning disorder.

The answer for both Jeff and Rob is, it depends. It is usually assumed that the verbal and the performance areas of an intelligence test are in fact measuring different facets of intelligence. In the case of Jeff, the score on the performance test might or might not be an appropriate measure of his underlying capability to master the content in the academic classroom. Rob's normal range scores on both the verbal and the performance scales could be masking extremely high verbal abilities and capabilities in the academic classroom.

The key word in diagnosis of learning disorder among students with varied ethnicity is *caution*. Unless you are the one who selects, administers, or selects and administers the intelligence and achievement tests, you are well advised to be cautious if asked to explain the results to parents or students.

The first interpretation of test results will probably come from another professional. But because you may be more likely to have continuing contact with the student and the parent, you could be asked to further explain or clarify the results. When reading the report from the school psychologist, look for evidence that ethnicity and sensory impairments were considered in measurement of both intelligence and achievement.

Be aware that there sometimes will be a very fine line between a student's being or not being diagnosed with a learning disorder. Having the diagnosis can result in additional resources being available. Having a *problem in learning* can be just as devastating, regardless of whether the criteria for specific learning disorder were met.

Primary Learning Disorders

The three primary learning or academic skills disorders are reading, mathematics, and written expression (the 3 Rs). In each case, the common feature is a level of achievement significantly below what would be expected from the student's level of intelligence. If a disorder of learning is diagnosed, the discrepancy between intelligence and achievement must not be the result of a history of poor academic instruction. As noted earlier, if there is a sensory impairment, the academic achievement problem must be greater than could be explained by the sensory difficulty alone.

The most important of the primary learning disorders is the condition identified as a reading disorder. It is the disabling academic skills condition that will have the most wide-ranging negative impact. In fact, when the criteria for one of the other learning disorders are met, there will most often be sufficient evidence to also diagnose a reading disorder.

Dyslexia is the general term for any disorder of reading, but definitions of that term will vary greatly, depending on the source. For example, a neuropsychological definition of dyslexia will typically focus on neurological, maturational, and genetic causes. Pedagogical definitions focus instead on the impact of different teaching methods. In popular usage, dyslexia is often associated only with input problems, without consideration of difficulties in comprehension.

When diagnosing the condition of dyslexia, the issues related to cause are put aside. A child or adolescent is defined as having the condition if, on appropriate individually administered tests of intelligence and achievement, there is a significant gap between the level of performance and the level expected from assessment of capability.

Reading disorders are usually not diagnosed until there has been at least 1 year of formal education. Males are much more likely to receive the diagnosis, but it is uncertain whether this is because of an actual genetic link or instead because the disorder often leads to problems in conduct, which lead to a referral for diagnosis.

As in all cases of diagnosis of a mental disorder, the condition must result in some impairment of function. Diagnostic coding systems typically assign a numerical value to each of the learning disorders. For example, the *DSM* code for reading disorder is 315.00. When either verbal or numerical codes are used for communication, it is important to remember that in diagnostic terminology, the term *dyslexia* is used much more broadly than just for a distortion in visual processing (e.g., letter reversal).

The learning disorders in mathematics and written expression use the same concept, differing only in the content in question. Typically, a diagnosis of mathematics disorder or disorder of written expression will not be made until after completion of first grade. Reading disorders are often diagnosed as early as the end of kindergarten. This is because it is reasonable to assume that reading skills will have been emphasized during the kindergarten year; mathematics and written expression may or may not have been.

Group achievement tests cannot be used for diagnosis of the learning disorder. In every case, the low level of achievement must be demonstrated through an individual assessment, and this complicates the early diagnosis of disorders of written expression. Many instruments are available for individual assessment in reading and mathematics. With the exception of spelling, standardized individual measures of written expression for the early school grades are not plentiful.

The importance of looking under the hood, so to speak, at the specific content used in the test was emphasized earlier in the chapter in reference to the measurement of intelligence. This can also be important when reviewing reports of measured achievement. For example, the reading score from one of the widely used tests of individual achievement includes no items associated with reading comprehension. It instead measures only the student's ability to correctly pronounce a series of individual words. As with the intelligence measures, continuing caution is warranted.

Does a Diagnosis of Learning Disorder Really Matter?

Given the controversy about the true nature of human intelligence, and the previously mentioned difficulties with the instruments used for measurement, one might wonder if this is worth the bother. Would a school counselor be better served through just avoiding the controversy, ignoring the presence or absence of a diagnosis of learning disorder?

This could be a tempting course of action. A strong argument could be made that every student who is experiencing academic achievement problems belongs in the scope of practice of the school counselor. Should it really matter whether the student meets the criteria for diagnosis with a learning disorder?

The perspective here is that it does matter, and the basis for that belief is that, when appropriately diagnosed, a condition of learning disorder has significant implications in the counselor's work with a student. We recognize that the skills associated with expertise on a football field, basketball court, or baseball diamond are not equally distributed among the population. There are underlying differences involving various biological systems that cannot be equalized through superior coaching.

There is increasing evidence that there are comparable differences in the human nervous system, that not all children are biologically equipped to process all forms of information with equal skill. Sometimes, the condition has global effect and is, as will be described below, diagnosed as mental retardation. In other instances, the processing impairment can be specific to certain forms of content. These are the learning disorders.

Biologically based learning disorders are not hopeless situations, but they do result in situations where some of the school guidance tools will not be sufficient. Of particular concern is your awareness that some activities, unless carefully structured, could in fact do harm.

Consider, for example, what would seem to be one of the most innocuous of activities: a group guidance activity designed to enhance study skills. Two students, both with normal range intelligence and both with poor mathematics achievement, are participating in this activity. If one of these students has a biologically based learning disorder, it is unlikely that this student's participation will result in more than a very slight gain in achievement. A peer, perhaps a friend, might very well experience a dramatic gain.

Assume that both students were highly motivated and both worked hard during the guidance activity. Unless you have prepared the student who has a learning disorder for a lower level of expectation from the activity, you may inadvertently have made a difficult situation even worse. How likely is it that the student with a learning disorder will then be able to find the motivation for a future activity better suited for the specific condition? For a student who likely is already struggling with feeling different, will a lack of success in the activity even further reinforce a feeling of being "damaged goods"?

It is crucial to remember that the *aspiration* or *expectancy effect* is a two-edged sword. There is no doubt that when teachers and counselors assume that a student cannot learn, the chances are increased that the student in fact will not learn. But when expectations are communicated that a student can learn with traditional stimuli in situations where there are biological explanations why the student actually cannot master the materials with those stimuli, our intervention has been harmful to the student. We said (or implied) that something could happen. When it does not, both the student's choices are bad. The student is likely to either blame him- or herself for the failure, or increase the extent of distrust in information from authority figures, or both.

The above is not intended to suggest a hopeless situation when a student has a learning disorder. Learning disorders have a biological basis in the nervous system, but then so does being nearsighted. Our need is for more and better information about the nature of the learning disorders and the appropriate forms of intervention. In the meantime, we need to be extremely cautious about the suggestion and recommendation of activities that might, despite our best intentions, exacerbate the effects of the condition.

Mental Retardation

In the multiaxial system, learning disorders are reported on Axis I. Mental retardation, however, is reported, along with personality disorders, on Axis II. This procedure reflects the likelihood that a condition of mental retardation will usually have an impact in a variety of different social, occupational, and academic settings.

Historically, a diagnosis of mental retardation was primarily based on the results of one of the major intelligence tests. An IQ score below 70 (with some margin for measurement error) was the primary criterion, along with some evidence of problems in adaptive function and an early onset. The IQ score was used to report the severity of the condition, with designation of profound, severe, moderate, or mild. More recently, the American Association for Mental Retardation has suggested a classification with more emphasis on the adaptation capabilities and a different scale for classifying the severity.

Diagnosis of mental retardation is a three-step process. The procedure begins with administration of one or more of the standard intelligence tests and a standardized adaptive skills test.

This is followed by preparation of a written description of individual strengths and weaknesses across the following four dimensions: (1) intellectual and adaptive behavior skills, (2) psychological/emotional features, (3) physical health conditions, and (4) environmental considerations. The standardized test data remain important in the diagnostic procedure but are used to provide only one part of a holistic assessment. Data for this written description assume a broad-based approach for information gathering, including interviews, observation, and direct interaction.

The third step in the diagnostic process is key in the recommended classification system. An interdisciplinary team considers all available data and, for each of the four dimensions, identifies the level of support that will be needed for optimal adaptive function.

Four categories of support are used in the diagnostic classification, as follows: intermittent, limited, extensive, and pervasive. In effect, this classification scheme places less emphasis on the level of the obtained IQ score and more emphasis on what is needed to maximize individual development.

Knowledge about the recommended procedures for diagnosis of mental retardation has possibly significant implications in the diagnosing of other learning disorders. First is the emphasis on what is needed rather than what is in deficit.

The level of intelligence, as measured by standard tests, is still a significant part of the diagnostic procedure. Persons with IQ scores significantly higher than 70 will not have the diagnosis of mental retardation regardless of the level of adaptive function; and there is recognition that a condition of mental retardation has one or more biological causes. But when the condition has been identified, the focus changes to what can be provided to help. In like manner, all disorders of learning that have a biological cause could possibly profit from use of a comparable perspective.

A second feature in diagnosis of mental retardation that warrants attention is another example of a situation in which harm can be inadvertently done while trying to do good. Both the historical and the more contemporary approaches to diagnosis of mental retardation assume that this is a condition that will be evident before age 18. Cognitive impairments that do not occur until after this age are not classified as mental retardation.

If it appears that a student is being misdiagnosed with mental retardation, school counselors and other professionals have often served as strong advocates for removing that label. When the interpretation of the performance on the intelligence measure is ignoring cultural or other features, the advocacy is certainly to be commended. If you find yourself in such a position, however, be aware that the stakes are high, and the cost of being wrong is large.

Typically, services for adults with mental retardation are made available through state agencies who are required to comply with specific guidelines to make the services available. If there is no diagnosis of mental retardation during the school years, the person with mental retardation may not be eligible for services as an adult. Thus, a well-intentioned effort to avoid such a label during the school years could result in needed services being denied when the student leaves the school setting. The effort directed toward not stigmatizing a given student at least sometimes would have been better directed at removing the stigma for the condition instead of removing the condition from the student.

Our next chapter continues the examination of cognitive disorders, with special attention to the diagnosis of attention-deficit/ hyperactivity disorder (ADHD). This topic warrants a separate chapter because the ADHD condition has become a catchword and a source of significant professional controversy.

A Quick Look Back

A test given covering the material in this chapter would anticipate that you are now better able to

1. Evaluate the appropriateness of an intelligence measure for use in identification of learning disorder
2. Identify the primary criteria for diagnosis of learning disorder
3. Discuss how cultural issues and sensory impairments should influence the diagnosis of learning disorder
4. Illustrate how lack of attention to learning disorders could result in a risk in the application of typical school guidance activity
5. Describe an approach to diagnosis of mental retardation that gives less emphasis to the IQ score

8

Attention Disorder Codes

BIOLOGY AND POLITICS

T here are few mental disorders that have received as much attention in the popular media as the condition of attention-deficit/
hyperactivity disorder (ADHD). Much of the controversy revolves
around concerns about the possibility of excessive use of medication,
often stated as a charge that we are drugging our children.

Despite the controversy, the criteria for diagnosing ADHD, at first
glance, appear very matter-of-fact. First, there must be evidence of a
persistent pattern of inattentiveness or a pattern of highly elevated
activity level, or both, that occurs with greater frequency and severity
than the age-level norm. Second, some symptoms of the condition
must have been present before age 7, even if the actual diagnosis is
made much later. Third, the inattentiveness or hyperactivity must
be evident in at least two different settings (e.g., home and school).

As usual, there also must be evidence that the symptoms are creating some impairment in coping and a better explanation for the symptoms (e.g., another mental disorder) must not be available.

With just three special criteria to be met, it might appear that this would be one of the easier conditions to diagnose. Appearances can be deceiving.

Boredom, Misbehavior, and Attention Disorder: Continuum or Categories?

Have you ever been bored? Could your behavior ever have been described as overactive? Did you ever (when you were a student) misbehave in an elementary school classroom?

A close examination of the three criteria for diagnosing ADHD suggests that one of the three, the multiple settings, would be generally easy to identify, and another, the onset before age 7, would be relatively easy to determine with an appropriate history. Deciding whether the inattentiveness or activity level is beyond normal range, though, can be extremely difficult.

To make the latter determination, you need extensive information about child development, and you need a great deal of information about a particular child. A high level of activity is the expected behavior for a healthy young child. Short attention span goes with the territory of childhood.

If ADHD is nothing more than the far end of a continuum of activity level and distractibility, then the intense feelings about not resorting to medication are easily understood. But if ADHD is in fact not on the continuum and instead is a truly different condition with a biological base, the arguments against medication seem hard to justify.

Is this a continuum or a distinct category? Consider the words of an adult describing the experience of this condition:

For me, having ADHD means I have an "input priority disorder." Everything within eye- or earshot takes on the same priority as the task I am supposed to be focused on. Even something simple, such as walking to the refrigerator for a drink, can become complicated or even lost in the shuffle of incoming stimulus. Each interruption puts me one task behind in completing the intended objective.

Another adult, who did not receive the ADHD diagnosis as a child, describes his experience with the prescribed medication: "The first day I took Ritalin, a thought came into my mind and I said, 'No. It isn't time for that now.' " Without the medication, he has trouble getting anything done. The smallest bit of incoming information, the quickest fleeting thought, or the slightest peep from a family member has the potential to derail him from whatever work he really should be doing, and he might not get back to the task at hand for hours, days, or weeks.

Adults often compare the use of medication to putting a new antenna on a radio. The medicine eliminates the constant static, distraction, and interference that had previously been a constant feature of life.

Children seldom have the depth of self-awareness to provide such an extensive self-analysis. If you have worked with a child who has ADHD, though, the parallels are obvious. Particularly striking is the suggestion that the condition makes it difficult (if not impossible) to put various sensory input into some priority order.

The Biology of Attention Disorders

There is increasing biological evidence that ADHD is a distinct category and not simply the extreme on a continuum of attention and activity. For example, a university research study, with children between the ages of 7 and 12, found an abnormal gene in children diagnosed with ADHD. This particular gene affects a hormone used by brain cells for the transmission of messages and was much more likely to be present in children with severe ADHD symptoms than in a control group.

A study of adults with attention-deficit symptoms, using positron emission tomography (PET) to scan the brain, found that these adults had lower than normal levels of activity in the areas of the brain that control concentration and the ability to get back on track after being distracted. Electroencephalograph (EEG) studies with children diagnosed with ADHD have found a higher than normal incidence of the brain wave patterns commonly associated with the sleep state rather than an attentive state.

Much remains to be learned about the biology of ADHD. The researchers who found the defective gene, for example, emphasized that this finding was not sufficient to fully explain the symptoms associated with this condition.

The data, however, clearly point to recognition that ADHD is a neurologically based syndrome with genetic features. The studies also provide some explanation for what had seemed a paradoxical effect in providing stimulants to so-called overstimulated children. It appears that, perhaps in a classic example of internal overreaction, the child with ADHD is attempting to compensate for a state of stimulation deficit. Stimulant medications (and perhaps other interventions as well) may serve to bring the internal stimulation into balance.

Diagnosing an Attention-Deficit/ Hyperactivity Disorder

The diagnostic process for ADHD is a multiple-stage process, beginning with a complete developmental history. Screening devices are available, to be completed by parents and teachers, to obtain information about the child's behavior in a variety of settings, particularly home and school. The diagnosis will typically also include administration of a battery of psychological tests, in part to rule out other conditions. A medical examination, including neurological screening, will also be included.

At the time of this writing, there is controversy about exactly what to call the disorder(s). The *DSM* uses a single descriptor for all conditions, child and adult. The disorder is identified as attention-deficit/ hyperactivity disorder. The diagnostic coding then continues with additional identification of one of three possible types: predominantly inattentive, predominantly hyperactive-impulsive, or combined.

A rationale for the single term *ADHD* is the belief that there is in fact only one condition, with symptoms often changing as the child matures. According to this belief, the hyperactivity component often diminishes at the time of adolescence.

There is sentiment among some to change the general label to attention-deficit disorder (ADD), followed by identification of whether ADD does or does not include hyperactivity-impulsivity. Without taking a position here on what the disorder(s) should be called, it does seem a bit incongruous to label a condition as ADHD when there is no evident hyperactivity.

Standard diagnostic procedure, then, is a review of various symptoms of inattentiveness, symptoms of hyperactivity, and symptoms of impulsiveness. A diagnosis of ADHD is made if (a) a sufficient number of those symptoms are evident at a higher rate than the age-appropriate norm, (b) the symptoms have persisted for at least 6 months, (c) the condition was evident before age 7, (d) the symptoms are exhibited in more than one setting, (e) the condition creates some impairment, and (f) the symptoms are not better explained by some other diagnosis.

That is the typical diagnostic procedure, but if, as appears likely from an increasing array of studies of brain function, ADHD is a condition distinct from overactivity, boredom, or both, this procedure may not be sufficient. What is needed, for example, in the area of inattentiveness, is not whether the child usually pays attention. An appropriate diagnosis instead requires information about how well it is actually possible for the child to stay on task. The better question is *can* rather than *does*.

Some computer-based screening tools have been developed that show promise for improved assessment of a child's maximum level of performance in maintaining attention and on-task behavior. Generalizing this assessment from an office to a classroom or home remains a difficult process.

The above concern is focused on the question of attentiveness. There could also be a question raised about the appropriateness of simply counting the symptom categories for assessment of hyperactivity and impulsivity; however, the determination of extreme levels of activity-impulsivity is usually not a difficult diagnostic decision. If there is any doubt about whether hyperactivity is present, then it probably is not. The behavior of a child with a biologically based ADHD leaves no question in your mind about these criteria. (The certainty of my opinion perhaps should be tempered by acknowledging that while typing these words, I see a still visible mark on my hand from an angelic-faced 6-year-old girl who bit me during an evaluation for ADHD 15 years ago.)

An increasing number of mental health professionals have suggested that many children diagnosed with ADHD instead actually have a condition that should have been identified as a childhood bipolar disorder. The symptoms are very similar, but ADHD tends to have earlier onset and be more chronic than episodic. Also suggested to help in differentiation is that a bipolar disorder in children often includes some psychotic features (e.g., imaginary persons). But, because imaginary playmates in young children are hardly an example of a mental disorder, this differentiation is difficult to apply.

School Politics and ADHD

There is often more than a little emotional intensity associated with opinions about the cause and best treatment of ADHD. Strong advocates can be found for a variety of different treatments, including medication, vitamins, allergy treatments, special diets, biofeedback, acupressure, and so forth. There does not appear to be a single best treatment for all children. For some children, medication seems to have resulted in dramatic improvement. Other children have experienced serious side effects from the use of medication, effects that can be more serious than the disorder itself.

There is also concern that ADHD (or ADD) is becoming a so-called fad disease (culturally induced ADHD). In fact, it is not difficult to find features in our society that seem to reinforce the symptoms of this disorder. Some examples include sound bites, the television remote control, e-mail, faxes, and so forth. A desire for a quick fix is often evident both within and outside the school setting.

A school counselor can be in a precarious position when making recommendations regarding this condition. Encouraging a parent to take the child to a physician for possible medication to control ADHD symptoms could destroy credibility with that parent and make it difficult to enlist the parent's support in other areas. Not encouraging the parent to take this action could have exactly the same effect.

Probably the best position in this (and also in many other instances) is to help parents become aware of a variety of alternatives and, to the greatest extent possible, be supportive of whatever decision the parents make. Encouraging the establishment of parent support groups can be extremely helpful. Parenting a child who has ADHD is difficult at best (a situation exacerbated by the likelihood that at least one of the parents may also have the condition).

A Strategy to Avoid Some Pitfalls

It can be difficult, especially because of the emotional intensity often associated with this diagnosis, to find the right words to communicate to parents the probable basis for ADHD. The following metaphor has often proven useful and has further served to encourage the parents to take steps for intervention. The concept is to use a common and nonthreatening condition (nearsightedness) to describe the impact and intervention possibilities for ADHD.

Being nearsighted is technically a nervous system disorder. Vision is a nervous system function, and a nearsighted person has a brain condition that prevents accurate focus. In the same spirit, biologically based ADHD is a nervous system disorder. Something in the brain is preventing satisfactory processing and control of incoming stimuli and outgoing behavior.

It is possible to treat nearsightedness in a so-called natural way through change in behaviors. A nearsighted child can be instructed to sit closer to the chalkboard, hold the book closer to the face, attempt to read only in bright light, and so forth. Many activities would be precluded but a nearsighted child could in fact get along fairly well under these circumstances.

Of course, no one would really consider such an approach. If a child is nearsighted, the child gets a prescription for glasses. Most often (if the glasses are worn), the outcome is equal opportunity with other children.

In like manner, a child with biologically based ADHD may be able to almost cope without so-called unnatural intervention. A biological intervention, most often a prescribed medication, could, like the glasses, provide equality with other children.

An advantage of this metaphor is that it can be used further in clarifying for the parents the media presentations about harmful effects of medication. Consider a child whose vision is 20-200 (very nearsighted). If that child's glasses are worn by a child who has 20-20 vision, the result is not sharper vision. The outcome is distorted reality.

Giving ADHD medication to a child who does not have a biologically based ADHD has that same kind of effect. The condition will become worse, not better.

This example provides a comforting rationale for a parent whose child might profit from medication. In addition, it allows you to strongly emphasize that there is a real distinction between biologically based ADHD and the circumstances when a child's inattentiveness and elevated activity level are behaviorally based.

In both cases, there is a need for intervention. This is a situation where accurate diagnostic coding is a crucial feature in selecting the appropriate intervention.

Until more is known about specific features of biologically based ADHD, there will continue to be instances in which the only way to make a determination may be through a brief trial with medication. Semantics can become crucial. Communicating that a brief medication trial is the final step in determining whether the ADHD symptoms have a biological base may be the same as "let's try a medication and see if it works." It may be the same thing, but it doesn't sound the same.

The next chapter is focused on the disorders often encountered among adolescents. Attention is given to the various issues that revolve around oppositional or aggressive behavior, eating disorders, and substance abuse disorders.

A Quick Look Back

A test covering the material in this chapter could expect you to

1. Defend a position on whether ADHD is on a continuum of activity and attention problems or instead is a distinct disorder
2. List the primary criteria used to identify ADHD
3. Discuss problems in obtaining accurate information for assessment of the criteria used to identify ADHD
4. Present a feasible hypothesis to explain why stimulants appear to have a reverse effect on children with ADHD
5. Discuss parallels between nearsightedness and ADHD, including rationale for intervention

Adolescent Codes

DEVELOPMENTAL STAGES
AND DEVELOPMENTAL DISASTERS

Although all the disorders described in the previous chapters can be found among adolescents, there are some additional conditions that can be especially troublesome in the school setting. Those conditions are the focus of this chapter. We begin with consideration of distress associated with conduct and misbehavior.

Rebellion during the adolescent years is of course not unusual. In fact, a case could be made for the belief that some degree of challenge to the values of the parents and other authorities is a desirable developmental activity during adolescence. There is often less risk to self and others when rebellion occurs during the teens instead of during the 20s or 30s. The conditions to be described first in this chapter are those, however, that go beyond the normal range.

Oppositional Defiant Disorder

A 13-year-old male student has been referred to you by one of his teachers. The note explaining the reason for the referral is, however, puzzling. It seems that the parent telephoned the teacher to ask about misbehavior at school, because his behavior at home has gradually become intolerable. He is argumentative, even hostile, toward both parents and an older brother. He refuses to do any of his assigned chores and seems to be deliberately finding ways to cause turmoil. Family activities have become almost impossible, to the extent that a planned family vacation may be canceled. It is now near the end of the school year, and this behavior has been going on since school started in the fall.

The puzzling part of this example is that this teacher has seen no evidence of this kind of behavior and in fact doesn't think the student has had problems in any of his classes. (I realize, by the way, that this would be an awfully long note from a teacher but needed all of that information to make some points that will follow.)

Before you see the student, you review his school record and talk with some of his other teachers. Everything seems fine. You then meet with the student and find no evidence of oppositional characteristics. He is polite, agreeable, and pleasant. He admits that things haven't been going especially well at home but insists that this is only because his parents are being so unreasonable.

This example was created deliberately to illustrate some of the difficult features in diagnosing an adolescent oppositional defiant disorder (which it appears that this young man probably has). He is a male, and this disorder occurs more often in males. It came on gradually, not suddenly. The problem behavior has lasted more than 6 months and seems to be beyond the boundaries of normal adolescent development. The behavior clearly seems to be creating some impairment in functioning in the home setting.

It is of course possible that the parents are the ones with a problem, not the young man. The specifics in this example, however, were chosen to illustrate that a diagnosis of oppositional defiant disorder might be completely appropriate even when you can see no evidence of it in the school setting.

Oppositional defiant disorder can be diagnosed in a child and usually appears no later than early adolescence. The symptoms are not necessarily evident in all settings and are actually most likely to be seen in interaction with adults with whom the adolescent feels safest. To make this diagnosis, there must be some impaired function but this would not necessarily have to be reflected in his school performance. Denying the disorder and instead attributing the problem to others is very typical.

Because there is no apparent impairment in the school setting, you would probably want to refer this case to an outside mental health professional. Someone would certainly need to confirm the severity of the symptoms before a diagnosis is made, but it would be prudent not to rush to judgment that the parents were simply overreacting.

The obvious key to the diagnosis of oppositional defiant disorder is in whether the rebellious behavior has gone outside the bounds of the normal range. This determination is not always an easy task and is often a very close call for the diagnostician.

You may also have noticed in the example a feature that can add to the difficulty of the decision: an older brother. It is very likely that the older brother's behavior provided the primary norm being used by the parent to decide that this truly was a problem. A special skill is sometimes necessary for the counselor to convince the parent that there might be more reason to be concerned about the oldest son's lack of rebellion than about the misbehavior of the younger son.

The importance of this diagnosis is the decision about whether an intervention is needed. If the misbehavior is within the boundaries of a normal developmental task in establishing identity, no intervention is necessary. Time may be all that is required to solve the problem.

If, however, the behavior is outside the normal boundaries, the assistance of a counselor is needed. The patterns of behavior being established will probably not go away without intervention. There is also risk of escalation into major conduct problems, some of which involve risk to the student or others.

Conduct Disorder

An adolescent who is diagnosed with a conduct disorder will have many things in common with the adolescent who has a diagnosis of oppositional defiant disorder. Both are likely to be disobedient and to rebel against authority figures. Both are more likely to be male. Could the young man in our example be diagnosed with a conduct disorder rather than oppositional defiant disorder?

Of course, the answer to the question is, it depends. The apparent lack of misbehavior in the school setting makes the diagnosis of conduct disorder less likely (but not impossible). Conduct disorder symptoms are evident in a variety of settings, not just in the home. Most often, if there is a conduct disorder, the problem will be having some impact on performance at school.

The information necessary to make the differential diagnosis in this case, though, has not been given. Conduct and oppositional disorders share the disobedience criteria, but students with conduct disorders will also be engaged in other, more serious activity. The critical feature in diagnosis of conduct disorder is a pattern of behavior with serious antisocial features. Examples include both behavior that results in physical harm (or threat) to others and behavior that results in property damage or theft.

To be diagnosed with a conduct disorder, there must be a persistent pattern of such behavior over time. An isolated incident of theft is diagnosed as antisocial behavior (Chapter 3). The aggressiveness of an adolescent with conduct disorder goes beyond a single, sometimes boundary-testing, occurrence.

Depending on your school setting, you may spend a significant amount of time with students whose behavior could be diagnosed as conduct disorder (when they are not suspended for truancy or breaking other school rules). More specific information about the actual form of misbehavior of our student in the example will be needed to rule out a conduct disorder, but the more serious diagnosis does not appear likely in this case.

This is a diagnostic condition in which cultural and environmental features warrant special attention before making the diagnosis and especially before planning an intervention. The environment around some schools is such that aggressive behavior that approaches or meets the criteria for conduct disorder can be a necessary coping tool for survival.

The student who lives in an at-risk neighborhood and the student whose home is in an upper-middle-class suburb may both warrant diagnosis of conduct disorder. Both could in fact share another common feature, frequently absent parents. For both of these students, there is a need for intervention. The very nature of the conduct disorder symptoms means that the student and others are at some risk.

The diagnosis for these two students may be the same, and the symptoms may be comparable. Intervention strategies must be more specific. For example, both would probably benefit from closer, more consistent supervision. For one of the students, that option would require only that the parents be willing to cooperate. For the other, that option is often just not available.

Although there clearly are major environmental considerations that result in the behaviors diagnosed as conduct disorders, there may be more. In addition to the obvious psychosocial features, there is evidence, from some adoption and twin studies, of a genetic contribution to the likelihood of development of conduct disorder.

When a diagnosis of conduct disorder is made, there is (as you're no doubt accustomed to by now) a requirement that the condition is not better described with another diagnosis. The V code for antisocial behavior, an adjustment disorder with disturbance of conduct, and the oppositional defiant disorder are among the alternatives that must be considered. When conduct disorder is diagnosed, additional explanation is given, including when it occurred (childhood or adolescence) and the severity of the symptoms (mild, moderate, or severe).

It is again important to emphasize the necessity of understanding the normal bounds of oppositional behavior. There are times, whether the observer is a parent or a teacher, when a report of oppositional behavior or disorderly conduct communicates more about the observer than about the student.

Substance Use and Abuse Disorders

Any listing of disorders of adolescence would be incomplete without consideration of substance (legal or illegal) abuse. There are, as you well know, strong and differing beliefs about how these conditions should be treated and how these problems could be prevented. Some would suggest a 12-Step program for essentially all adolescents; some argue that legalizing use by adults would make it much easier to identify and provide treatment for adolescents who are substance abusers. Specialty certification for counselors goes by various titles, including substance abuse counselor, alcohol and drug counseling, and certified addictions counselor. There is either increasing or decreasing use of illegal substances by adolescents, depending on which survey you read. There is little consensus on the actual extent of drug use by the adolescent population.

Despite the disparity in beliefs about cause, best treatment, and actual incidence, no one would argue that the problem of drug use among adolescents is inconsequential. For society and for the individuals and families involved, the impact of substance abuse can be devastating.

Despite the other areas of controversy, the diagnostic process essentially is simply to identify the substance(s) along with the extent to which there is resulting impairment in everyday function. In the *DSM* coding system, for example, there are two primary categories, as follows: (1) disorders that are "induced" by a substance and (2) disorders that are defined by use of the substance.

Although in most instances, the diagnostic codes are used to identify and describe a condition without attributing the cause, we have encountered periodic exceptions to the rule. The diagnosis of adjustment disorder was one of the exceptions. Substance-induced disorders are another example of the diagnosis providing both condition and probable cause.

A student is referred to you and reports all of the symptoms associated with a generalized anxiety disorder (GAD). If you also learn that the student is inappropriately using amphetamines, GAD may not be the appropriate diagnosis. There is instead a specific diagnostic category and numerical code to identify a diagnosis of amphetamine-induced anxiety disorder. Comparable codes are available for various substances and conditions (i.e., alcohol-induced mood disorder, cannabis-induced psychotic disorder, and so forth).

When there is no evidence of another disorder induced by the substance use, the diagnosis is used instead to just identify the use of the substance. The *DSM* system uses the two following categories: (1) substance dependence and (2) substance abuse. Substance dependence is the more severe of these conditions. Diagnosis includes identification of the substance and also provides for additional identification of (a) whether there is physiological as well as psychological dependence and (b) an assessment of the present status (i.e., full remission, partial remission, and so forth).

Obtaining accurate information is the critical feature in diagnosis of substance-related disorders. Among adolescents, denial of use (or impact) is the typical response. When reasonably dependable information can be obtained from the adolescent, peers, or family, the diagnosis of the substance-related disorders is not complex. Substances included, by the way, are not only those most often associated with drug abuse (alcohol, cannabis, cocaine, and so forth). Caffeine and nicotine are also included as substances to which an impairing dependence can be evident.

Eating Disorders

A variety of different problems associated with weight and appearance occur during adolescence. The three primary diagnostic categories for eating disorders that may appear during the adolescent years are anorexia (anorexia nervosa), bulimia (bulimia nervosa), and binge eating disorder. Some of the common symptoms of the eating disorders are provided in Table 9.1.

TABLE 9.1 Typical Symptoms of Eating Disorders

	Anorexia	Bulimia	Binge Eating
Abuse of drugs or alcohol		X	X
Binge eating without weight gain		X	
Eating in secret	X	X	X
Excessive weight loss in short time	X		
Feelings of helplessness	X	X	X
Loss of monthly menstrual periods	X	X	
Low self-esteem	X	X	X
Obesity	X		
Obsession with exercise	X	X	
Unusual eating rituals	X	X	

The National Institute of Mental Health (NIMH) suggests that approximately 1% of adolescent girls can be diagnosed with anorexia. Although this may seem a relatively small incidence rate, if you have 200 adolescent females in your work assignment as a school counselor, you could expect that 2 of these students have this life-threatening condition. Those students experience the distress of feeling fat, despite being at least 15% below the appropriate weight for their height and bone structure. The roots of anorexia are in a distorted view of weight, food, and body image. Consider the following example:

You have an appointment with a student, Alice, to plan the course schedule for her senior year. You remember her from previous encounters as a bright, eager-to-please, young woman who was slightly overweight.

When she comes into your office, you are startled at her emaciated appearance. When questioned, she first denies that there is any problem but eventually acknowledges that she has been dieting for "a while." It started innocently enough. Someone suggested that she would have more dates if she lost some weight. But, as the pounds began to come off, she became obsessed with the weight loss, began exercising compulsively, and developed strange eating rituals to reduce the daily food intake. Her menstrual periods have stopped. She is physically weak. She is terrified at the thought of gaining weight. If you attempt to help her understand that she has lost too much weight, she will deny vigorously and escape your office as quickly as possible.

Alice's situation is not unusual, including the fact that she came to your office only because of a need involving course scheduling. Students with anorexia will seldom come to your attention as a result of being problem students. On the contrary, their behavior is more often near perfection. They are good students, seldom disobey, and tend to keep their feelings to themselves. You have to *notice* them. They will neither acknowledge this condition nor seek help for it from you.

When diagnosing the anorexic condition, although the student may deny the problem, you do have visible physical signs. Diagnosing bulimia is more difficult because the student with the bulimic condition is typically of average weight.

The bulimic diagnosis is defined by episodes of binge eating followed by some form of purging behavior. Vomiting is the most typical purging behavior, but there are other forms, including excessive laxatives, diuretics, and even fasting or excessive exercise. The NIMH suggests an even higher incidence rate for bulimia than for the anorexic condition, approximately 2% to 3% of young women.

Peggy, another student for whom you are the assigned counselor, also has an eating disorder that began with just wanting to lose weight. In addition, she had been trying to cope with feelings of loneliness, anger, and fear. When the feelings became overwhelming, she experienced an uncontrollable desire for sweet food. She would eat literally pounds of candy and cake, stopping only when she was either exhausted or in severe pain. Then, overcome with guilt and shame, she would make herself vomit.

Over time this became a pattern of behavior, binge and then purge. She felt powerless to stop the behavior but carefully kept it a secret.

A bulimic condition, like anorexia, typically begins during adolescence. Even close family and friends have difficulty detecting the disorder, even though the binge-and-purge cycle can occur as often as several times a day. Unless it is uncovered as a result of some other behavior, for example a suicide attempt, many individuals with bulimia, ashamed of the habit, do not seek help until in their 30s or 40s.

The condition diagnosed as binge eating disorder has much in common with bulimia. There are frequent episodes of uncontrolled eating. Persons with this disorder eat large quantities of food in a single sitting, not stopping until they are uncomfortably full. Obesity is common, however, because the binge eating is not followed by purging. It is estimated that approximately 2% of the population could be diagnosed with binge eating disorder.

Although each of these three diagnostic conditions is more prevalent in females, the disorders are not limited by gender. Each of the three conditions results in increased risk of medical complications; the physical damage associated with anorexia and bulimia is especially serious. A concurrent diagnosis of depressive disorder (co-morbidity) is also a common feature of the eating disorders.

If you suspect an eating disorder, encouraging a referral for a complete physical examination is crucial. Some of the newer antidepression medications appear to be helpful in controlling the symptoms. A hospital-based treatment program will sometimes be necessary.

As a school counselor, you can have an especially important role in encouraging the student to start and stay with a treatment program. Demonstrating that you truly care, providing information about the dangers of eating disorders, and convincing the student to get help could literally result in the saving of a life.

Wrapping It Up

This ends our tour and discussion of the diagnosis of conditions selected as most likely to be encountered in the work of the school counselor. In the final chapter, we will look at some of the alternative diagnostic models and provide suggestions about diagnosis of conditions not specifically addressed in this book. We will also attempt some "future thought," exploring some ideas about why (or whether) a school counselor can expect more or less emphasis on diagnostic coding and in what form. Before moving to that discussion, from this chapter, it is anticipated that you are able (or better able) to

1. Identify key characteristics of an oppositional defiant disorder
2. Identify key characteristics of a conduct disorder
3. Discuss the significance of cultural and socioeconomic features in diagnosis of conduct and oppositional disorders
4. Differentiate among the three primary categories of eating disorders
5. Describe how the *DSM* categorizes disorders of substance use and abuse

Diagnostic Codes
IS THIS ALL THERE IS?

O ur focus in this book has been on the diagnostic conditions that
are more likely to be found among students in the school-age
population. Although the conditions we have discussed are the most
common, they are certainly not the only diagnosable problems to be
found in students. We begin this chapter with a few examples of other
conditions and with suggestions about how to search for information
about the diagnostic codes we have not covered in detail.

Where Are the
Rest of the Disorders?

There are a number of other mental disorders associated with
childhood and adolescence that you might encounter during your

career. Just a few examples include Tourette's syndrome (a condition characterized by sudden, rapid, recurrent, stereotyped motor movement and/or vocalization), enuresis (lack of bladder control without primary physical cause), autistic disorder (a severe condition that precludes normal levels of social interaction), and childhood schizophrenia (a severe psychotic condition characterized by delusions, hallucinations, and lack of contact with reality).

The general diagnostic process for these and other disorders involves the same steps we have used in diagnosis of other conditions. First, there must be evidence that the symptoms are resulting in impairment of the student's ability to cope with everyday demands. In multiaxial terms, this is the GAF, and you may have already now recognized why a bottom-up approach for multiaxial assessment was suggested in Chapter 2. Typically, regardless of the symptoms, if the GAF is high, there is no disorder to diagnosis.

Assuming that the symptoms are causing some impairment in functioning, the next step is a combination of identifying and ruling out other explanations for the symptoms. Psychosocial features are reported on Axis IV. Medical conditions that may contribute to the symptoms are reported on Axis III. Persistent patterns of behavior or conditions that may create the symptoms in a variety of settings are reported on Axis II. Finally, what will usually be the primary focus of treatment is identified on Axis I.

Usually, the diagnosis on Axis I will be the identification of the most severe disorder necessary to explain the symptoms. If you know the name for the probable disorder, the manual for the diagnostic system you are using, for example, the *DSM*, is consulted to attach the numerical code and perhaps confirm that the symptom criteria have been met. When the name of the disorder is not known, which is likely to be the case for the unusual conditions, you consult the manual and search for the name of the disorder by using the symptoms. In either instance, you have first made an assessment of the extent to which the symptoms are making it difficult for the student to cope and you have considered hypotheses other than a mental disorder that could explain those symptoms.

What About the
Alternatives to the *DSM*?

Most, though not all, examples of diagnostic coding in this book are consistent with the *Diagnostic and Statistical Manual for Mental Disorders*, prepared by the American Psychiatric Association. As has been noted before, the *DSM* is the primary resource for diagnosis in a wide range of settings.

There are, however, other approaches to diagnosis. Some members of the American Counseling Association, for example, have stated concerns about the underlying premise of the *DSM* model and have suggested the creation or use of other diagnostic systems, which, they believe, would be more congruent with the philosophy of counseling. Representatives of other professional groups have made similar recommendations, and it would in fact be a mistake to assume that all psychiatrists would give unconditional endorsement to the *DSM*.

An extensive review here of the alternative diagnostic models proposed would go far beyond the intended scope of this book (and I would still be at risk of perhaps skipping your personal favorite among them). Instead, we will use three of the alternative models to illustrate how and to what extent other available approaches to diagnosis may differ from the *DSM*.

The simplest of the alternatives to *DSM* coding is the classification scheme developed by the World Health Organization. In its 10th revision, the system is titled the *International Statistical Classification of Diseases and Related Health Problems* (ICD-10). ICD numerical codes for the medical disorders are sometimes reported on Axis III in multiaxial systems. In the latest revision, the mental disorders section of the *ICD-10* was coordinated with the *DSM* to make the two systems compatible.

Thus, the same *diagnosis* would be given in *ICD-10* and *DSM* systems. The difference is in the number code assigned to that diagnosis. For example, a *DSM* diagnosis of dysthymic disorder, 300.4, is the same as an *ICD-10* diagnosis of dysthymic disorder, F34.1.

Because the *ICD-10* and *DSM* systems are so comparable when identifying mental disorders, you might wonder why the former warrants mention here. It is anticipated that, at some point, use of the *ICD-10* numerical codes will be a mandated requirement for government reports related to mental disorders. When this occurs, it is likely that the requirement will generalize to billing of insurance companies and managed-care activities.

The *ICD* system is, obviously, little different from the *DSM* approach. A diagnostic alternative suggested by Allen Ivey is very different. The approach he recommends has received some attention, particularly within the counseling profession.

The Ivey model, referred to as Developmental Counseling and Therapy (DCT), was designed to integrate neo-Piagetian developmental theory into the counseling process. Piaget suggested that cognitive development proceeds through a series of discrete stages, as follows: sensorimotor, preoperational, concrete operations, and formal operations. The DCT model makes some adaptation in definitions of the stages. The preoperational stage is termed as late sensorimotor, and an additional level, postformal operations, is added. In essence, though, the model claims roots in the rich Piagetian tradition.

A counselor applying the DCT diagnostic approach will identify and assess the level of cognitive development evident throughout a counseling interview and then take steps to expand the level either *horizontally* or *vertically*. For example, a child operating in the counseling session at the concrete level could be encouraged to go further in discussion at this cognitive level (horizontal expansion). The child instead could be encouraged to vertically expand with more consideration of feelings (down to a sensorimotor level) or vertically expand upward to work in the Piaget level of formal operations. Diagnosis in the DCT model is the identification of the cognitive levels as they change within and between counseling sessions.

This model may be vulnerable to criticism that the principles of cognitive development, associated with the work of Piaget, are stretched past a reasonable limit when applied in this fashion. Some would argue, for example, that there is reason to question whether most elementary school children are neurobiologically capable of cognitive operation higher than the concrete level.

The DCT model, however, is intuitively satisfying to many counselors because of its primary emphasis on the concept of development. Ivey and his colleagues have provided research data that seem to support some efficacy in this approach.

Still another approach to diagnosis is focused not on the content of the counseling process but on the degree to which a *readiness for change* is evident in the student. James Prochaska and his colleagues, in a model called the transtheoretical approach, suggested that there are four identifiable stages through which the student will pass if successful in dealing with the kinds of problems that warrant counseling.

The first stage is called *precontemplation*. Students in this stage might be in your office because they were required to be there but would not acknowledge a need for counseling. During the next stage, *contemplation*, the student has acknowledged that a problem exists and is weighing the pros and cons of making the necessary change in behavior. Actual behavior change and problem resolution occur in the *action* stage. The final stage in this model is *maintenance*. In this last stage, the gains are solidified and plans are made between counselor and student to maintain and continue the positive outcomes. Identifying the present stage of the student is the diagnosis in their transtheoretical model.

Although in some instances there would seem to be difficulty in integration of this model with applications of brief therapy, this four-stage model has empirical support. An accurate diagnosis using this model would appear of particular benefit to the counselor in planning for the counseling session.

The examples above were selected to be illustrative of some of the available alternatives to the *DSM* diagnostic model. In comparison to the *DSM* approach, the *ICD* model differs only in what number to assign to the diagnosis. The DCT is focused on what is going on in the counseling session, and the transtheoretical model diagnoses where a student is in the process of behavior change.

It's interesting, and perhaps relevant, that the proponents of alternatives to the *DSM* system tend to be profession-specific. Psychologists are not prone to suggest that counselors need a unique coding system. Counselors do not rush to suggest that both the American

Counseling Association (ACA) and the National Association of Social Workers should have their own codes. The need for new coding systems, among the professional groups, is often supported by statements that what *we do* is too important and too philosophically different to be captured with the dominant system.

There is no question that the *DSM* is an imperfect system. We have seen examples throughout this book not only of conditions in which the terminology can be misleading but also of situations in which there is a great deal of subjectivity in the distinctions made between some disorders. Through selection of what should and should not be identified as a mental disorder (e.g., homosexuality), the *DSM* has at times been a diagnostic instrument with highly political overtones.

There is also, I believe, no doubt that the exclusive use within a professional group of any alternative diagnostic system would destroy the primary value of the diagnostic codes. There perhaps might be gain in the communication *within* a professional group, but it would be at a huge cost in loss of communication among the different groups.

Granting, for example, the possibility that counselors could create a system that was more consistent than the *DSM* with the philosophical underpinnings of the profession, and assuming that this new system was endorsed by the ACA and became widely used by counselors, we would create a greater problem than the one we solved. The new system might possibly facilitate communication among counselors but would most likely impair communication with the large number of others who have shared interest and concern. That is the best-case scenario, assuming that a more congruent system could in fact be created and endorsed by most counseling specialties.

As noted earlier in this book, even with all of its flaws, the problem-focused approach of the *DSM* enhances the likelihood of accurate communication among professional groups. We can differ on why the problem exists and what should be done to relieve it. We can even differ on whether something actually is a problem. But we remain on the same page, so to speak, in defining the problem we are talking about.

The difficulty with alternative systems may actually just be in the word *alternative*. There are marked differences, for example, in *what is being diagnosed* among the *DSM*, DCT, and transtheoretical models. But are these approaches incompatible or just different?

Consider an intervention with a student who is experiencing distress related to the relationship with a particular teacher. The *DSM* model allows you to identify the extent and type of distress. The transtheoretical model identifies whether the student is ready to make the changes necessary to remedy the distress. The DCT model might allow you to better understand and select interventions during the counseling session. Each diagnosis provides information that could help you in intervention with this student. This situation seems akin to a multiple-choice test item in which the best answer might be "all of the above."

What If We All Used Diagnostic Codes?

A brief venture into the future seems a worthy endeavor before we come to an end. There has been a continuing theme throughout this book that the concepts in diagnostic coding are consistent with what school counselors do. The diagnostic codes have been shown to be frequently applicable to the kinds of problems in students served by the counselors.

Unsaid, to this point, has been the fact that diagnostic coding is not now being used in the school setting to nearly the same extent as is found in many other counseling specialties. If the codes were already in wide use in school counseling, this book would have been unnecessary. Familiarity and ease with the diagnostic codes would have been a prerequisite for employment as a school counselor.

The "what if" in this section will be addressed from two different directions, one positive, one negative, both of which seem within the realm of possibility. We will first look at what might happen if we began to routinely use the diagnostic codes in the practice of school counseling (I think it would be positive), and then consider an unpleasant possibility of being forced to use the codes.

Beginning with the more pleasant of these possibilities, a movement within the school counseling profession to begin extensive use of the diagnostic coding systems would have several positive benefits. First is the advantage emphasized throughout this book: more effective communication.

All school counselors work with students who have problems with elevated anxiety. It is evident in the elementary school student who claims to be ill each morning to avoid going to school, and it is evident in the secondary school student frightened about what to do after graduation. Excessive anxiety can be a concern when working with an individual student, or it can involve an entire group of students, for example, after a natural disaster.

The communication problem is in our use of the language. The student you would describe as being "highly anxious" and the student I would identify as "highly anxious" might very well have significantly different levels of anxiety. When we then consult about such students and how best to help them, our differences in use of the terms may preclude effective communication.

Consider the difference if, as an example, you identified the problems faced by your student as an adjustment disorder with anxious mood, and I described the problems faced by my student as generalized anxiety disorder. With the more precise use of the terms, we might be much better able to share thoughts about experiences with comparable students and identify the kinds of interventions most likely to be successful.

It isn't that the *DSM* is necessarily right in how problems are identified. It is instead that it provides a common vocabulary with known definitions. We are thus speaking the same language.

Remember the example from Chapter 1, the mental health professional who described a student's condition and status to the school counselor, using the diagnostic vocabulary. A reversal of that process would most likely result in a significant improvement in the diagnostic activity. If the school counselor were to make the referral, with an explanation that it appears to be an adjustment disorder with also some behaviors suggesting a borderline personality disorder, there is significantly increased likelihood of an accurate diagnostic determination. The referral source would be alerted and could well use the observations and expertise that the school counselor brings to understanding the needs of a given student.

Possible advantages of wide use of the diagnostic codes in the context of school counseling certainly include the applications in individual counseling, but there are other possibilities as well. Think for a moment about your favorite group guidance activity, a program that you use frequently and may have even designed or adapted yourself. Now ask yourself, does this activity work for all the students with whom it is used?

The answer (unless you have created a truly remarkable program) is, of course, that it works well with most students; otherwise, it wouldn't be your favorite. But there are some students the activity doesn't reach. Who are they?

I believe data would support that, in many cases, the students whose needs are not being met will share a common diagnostic condition. One obvious example was used earlier in the book, the effect of study skills activities on students with true learning disorders.

Imagine the development of an activity designed to enhance feelings of self-efficacy. Imagine further that this activity works very well with students who have the problems identified as adjustment disorder with depressed mood but does not work well with students with more severe depressive conditions or with students whose symptoms of adjustment are primarily in the form of anxiety.

Now, consider that you've used this activity with a mixed group of students, perhaps with about equal representation from each of these three diagnostic conditions. When you evaluate the effectiveness of the activity, the total group data would probably suggest that the activity was a failure. Evaluating that same activity while making use of the additional information from the diagnostic codes would not only demonstrate the success with a specified problem area but also could provide clues about what modifications to make in light of the needs of students with other diagnostic conditions.

There is, unfortunately, another side to the "what if" question. What if the use of diagnostic coding by school counselors were to be forced by an outside pressure?

A precedent from other counseling specialty areas has already occurred. It hasn't been long ago that counselors who worked in community- or state-funded agencies had little concern about third-party payment. The funding for the support of the agency was provided in lump sum by the community, the state, the federal government, or some combination of these sources.

As these words are being written, that is no longer the case in many agencies. The level of general support has either been reduced or has not been increased to meet the financial demands. Now, it is not unusual for the counselor in an agency to be expected to bill an insurer for individual or group counseling whenever a third-party payment may be available. The funds generated by the billing are a part of what allows the agency to continue operating.

Although one could hope that this scenario would not be duplicated in the school setting, the possibility cannot be totally discounted. School budgets are also shrinking in many places, and continued support for the services provided by school counselors can be at risk when budgets are cut. Billing for mental health services provided in the school setting is a concept that, for most of us, probably is not easily swallowed; but, especially given the precedent in the agencies, it could happen.

A school board, faced with extreme budget pressures, could inform the counselors in the district that they were to continue doing their jobs as presently defined, but also insist that all work that could result in reimbursement would be billed to the insurer. Funds generated would be used to support the overall counseling program. If such a scenario were to occur in your school system, the use of the diagnostic codes would, of course, no longer be a choice. Diagnostic coding is mandated.

A Final Thought

Throughout this book, there have been sometimes subtle and sometimes quite overt attempts at persuasive messages regarding the value in using the diagnostic codes. As we come to the end, I want to acknowledge and address a perception that often emerges when considering the use of diagnostic systems. In essence, this perception is that diagnosis is equal to labeling, and labeling is an activity to be avoided at all costs.

In Chapter 1, there was emphasis on the importance of thinking of a mental disorder as something a student *has*, not something a student *is*. An important way to reduce the possibility that diagnosis will inadvertently result in a harmful labeling of the student is to be sure that *has* is inserted as you think about and talk about a student's diagnostic condition.

It could, though, be alleged that an easier way to avoid the potential risk of diagnostic labeling would be to just *avoid* the diagnosis. Is this really a better (or even feasible) idea?

If you read my biography when you began this book, think back to that time and what your thoughts were as you went through the material. I am a college professor. I was a school counselor. I conduct diagnostic evaluations. Most likely, each of those statements produced some expectations about what might be in this book. Whether those expectations were more positive, more negative, or neutral was most likely dependent on your prior experiences with college professors, school counselors, and diagnosticians. My point is that this process of categorization with expectancy is inevitable. This is not a challenge to your objectivity. It is the way we process and store information.

You could go through your professional life without ever thinking in terms of an oppositional defiant disorder. But you cannot escape the automatic sorting of behaviors into categories. The advantage of a category such as oppositional defiant disorder, as opposed to smart-aleck brat or even behaviorally challenged young person, is that the category has been operationally defined.

Just as was the case when you were forming expectations about this book, there is no problem as long as the expectation is treated as a hypothesis to be later confirmed or disputed. Some form of categorization (labeling) is going to be evident when you are thinking about the students you serve.

The task is twofold. You want to be sure that the categorizations are not used in a form that is harmful to the student. And you want to be sure that the impressions are always viewed as only hypothetical, which may or may not be confirmed with additional information. When those two conditions are met, the question about labeling becomes moot.

With those conditions met, diagnostic codes can then effect sharper and more effective communication with your colleagues. On a broader scale, the appropriate coding can improve the extent to which research studies can provide data relevant for your practice, identifying what kinds of interventions in the school setting will work best with what kinds of problems.

Perhaps most important, when properly used, the diagnostic codes can enhance the way we think about the problems faced by our students. In thinking about how I wanted to end this book, I decided that an appropriate closure would be an acknowledgment of the belief that the diagnostic conditions described in it are "the enemy." The specificity and shared definitions allowed by the diagnostic codes give us the opportunity not only to conceptualize those conditions as adversaries but also to share ideas, thoughts, and tools that could eventually make these conditions less prevalent.

Appendix
SOME USEFUL RESOURCES

American Psychiatric Association. (1994). *Diagnostic and statistical manual of mental disorders* (4th ed.). Washington, DC: Author.

The DSM is the most widely used coding system for mental and behavioral disorders. This resource provides an exhaustive list of disorders, codes, and diagnostic criteria. Also included is extensive information regarding the history and preparation of the DSM multi-axial system.

Berkow, R. (Ed.). (1992). *The Merck manual of diagnosis and therapy* (16th ed.). Rahway, NJ: Merck Sharpe & Dohme Research Laboratories.

This manual, revised and published periodically by a pharmaceutical company, provides an encyclopedic resource of medical conditions in language for the layperson. Mental disorders are included, but this manual may be most useful as a quick resource for information about the possible influence of medical disorders. A free version of the manual is available on the Internet.

Costa, P. T., & Widiger, T. A. (Eds.). (1994). *Personality disorders and the five-factor model of personality.* Washington, DC: American Psychological Association.

> *This is a collection of theoretical and empirical studies regarding the nature and treatment of personality disorders. The chapters on how personality disorders could be used to guide selection of intervention strategies may be especially helpful.*

Ivey, Allen. (1986). *Developmental theory: Counseling into practice.* San Francisco: Jossey-Bass.

> *This book details the development and use of an alternative model of diagnosis, with emphasis on interview analysis. The system is rooted in the Piagetian stages of cognitive development.*

Preston, J., & Johnson, J. (1994). *Clinical psychopharmacology made ridiculously simple.* Miami: MedMaster.

> *This short (45-page) volume was written by a psychologist and a psychiatrist. The format is user-friendly, and there is a remarkably complete description of widely used psychotropics for a variety of mental disorders. Indications and contraindications for use of medications are included.*

Prochaska, J. O., & Diclemente, C. C. (1984). *The Transtheoretical approach: Crossing traditional boundaries of therapy.* Homewood, IL: Dow Jones-Irwin.

> *This resource describes the rationale and use of the stages of change diagnostic model. The model detailed in this book has subsequently been applied in a variety of studies regarding counseling outcomes.*

Seligman, L. (1986). *Diagnosis and treatment planning in counseling.* New York: Human Sciences Press.

> *This is an excellent resource for examples of how diagnostic concepts can be applied in the practice of counseling. It is designed for counselors and other nonmedical mental health professionals.*

World Health Organization. (1994). *International Statistical Classification of Diseases and Related Health Problems* (10th rev.). Geneva: Author.

This ICD manual provides diagnostic identification and codes for physical and mental disorders. The mental disorders section parallels the DSM but uses different alphanumeric codes for the disorders.

Index

CORWIN
PRESS

The Corwin Press logo—a raven striding across an open book—represents the happy union of courage and learning. We are a professional-level publisher of books and journals for K-12 educators, and we are committed to creating and providing resources that embody these qualities. Corwin's motto is "Success for All Learners."

Printed in the United States
41401LVS00002B/26

9 780803 964730